Until 2006, Margaret Wither
Evangelism among Children,
heightening the profile of children and the need to reach a new
generation with the gospel message. Formerly a music teacher in
several Inner London schools and for the Open University, she
became Diocesan Children's Adviser for Rochester in 1989. She
became heavily involved in providing training and support for
voluntary children's leaders in parishes and in 1996, while
Children's Officer for the Diocese of Chelmsford, she established
children's work as an integral part of Reader training as well as
providing a similar input to several theological courses. The
increasing demand for simple basic training for inexperienced
leaders led to her writing a four-evening course for a group of
parishes in 1998. This formed the basis of her book, *Fired Up... Not
Burnt Out* (Barnabas, 2001). She is also author of *The Gifts of
Baptism*, *Welcome to the Lord's Table* and *Where are the Children?*, all
published by Barnabas. Margaret is currently a freelance consultant,
working as an Associate of the Barnabas ministry team.

Tim Sledge is the Mission Enabler for the Diocese of Peterborough.
Before this, he was vicar of three parishes near Halifax. He has a
rich and varied Christian story, thoroughly embracing evangelical,
charismatic and catholic traditions, so he is also able to fit in and
communicate with people across the Anglican spectrum. Before
ordination, Tim worked for several years promoting music and
arts festivals, including the York Early Music Festival and the
Huddersfield Contemporary Music Festival. Tim is co-author of
Youth Emmaus 1 & 2 (CHP, 2003, 2006) and *Mission-Shaped Parish*
(CHP, 2006).

Text copyright © Margaret Withers and Tim Sledge 2008
Illustrations copyright © Ann Kronheimer 2008
The authors assert the moral right
to be identified as the authors of this work

Published by
The Bible Reading Fellowship
15 The Chambers, Vineyard
Abingdon OX14 3FE
United Kingdom
Website: www.brf.org.uk

ISBN 978 1 84101 533 0
First published 2008
10 9 8 7 6 5 4 3 2 1 0

Acknowledgments
Unless otherwise stated, scripture quotations are taken from the Contemporary English Version
of the Bible published by HarperCollins Publishers, copyright © 1991, 1992, 1995 American
Bible Society.

Scripture quotations from The New Revised Standard of the Bible, Anglicized Edition, copyright
© 1989, 1995 by the Division of Christian Education of the National Council of the Churches
of Christ in the United States of America, are used by permission. All rights reserved.

Scripture quotations taken from the Holy Bible, New International Version, copyright © 1973,
1978, 1984 by International Bible Society. Used by permission of Hodder & Stoughton
Publishers, a division of Hodder Headline Ltd. All rights reserved. 'NIV' is a registered
trademark of International Bible Society. UK trademark number 1448790.

Eucharistic Prayer H from *Common Worship, Services and Prayers for the Church of England*, is
copyright © The Archbishops' Council 2000 and reproduced by permission.

Performance and copyright
The right to perform *Creative Communion* drama material is included in the purchase price, so
long as the performance is in an amateur context, for instance in church services, schools or
holiday club venues. Where any charge is made to audiences, written permission must be
obtained from the author, who can be contacted through the publishers. A fee or royalties may
be payable for the right to perform the script in that context.

A catalogue record for this book is available from the British Library

Printed in Singapore by Craft Print International Ltd

Creative
Communion

Engaging the whole church in a journey of faith

Margaret Withers and Tim Sledge

Acknowledgment

*Thanks to our editor, Sue Doggett, for her vision
and for keeping us to our deadlines!*

Important information

Photocopying permission

The right to photocopy material in *Creative Communion* is granted for the pages that contain the photocopying clause: 'Reproduced with permission from *Creative Communion* published by BRF 2008 (978 1 84101 533 0), so long as reproduction is for use in a teaching situation by the original purchaser. The right to photocopy material is not granted for anyone other than the original purchaser without written permission from BRF.

The Copyright Licensing Agency (CLA)

If you are resident in the UK and you have a photocopying licence with the Copyright Licensing Agency (CLA), please check the terms of your licence. If your photocopying request falls within the terms of your licence, you may proceed without seeking further permission. If your request exceeds the terms of your CLA licence, please contact the CLA directly with your request. Copyright Licensing Agency, 90 Tottenham Court Rd, London W1T 4LP. Tel 020 7631 5555; fax 020 7631 5500; email cla@cla.co.uk; web www.cla.co.uk. The CLA will provide photocopying authorization and royalty fee information on behalf of BRF.

BRF is a Registered Charity (No. 233280)

Contents

✤

Foreword

The past ten years have seen something of a revolution in the thinking and practice surrounding eucharistic worship. The admission of baptized children to Holy Communion before confirmation has become firmly established and is growing steadily throughout the Anglican Church. Alongside this, our liturgy has moved from being text-bound to structure-based, with the potential for great flexibility within a common framework.

These exciting developments have led to many questions, such as:

• How do we celebrate Holy Communion in a way that is genuinely multi-generational?
• How can we best use the wealth of resources available?
• How might we engage all the senses in worship?
• How do we help form our young people as eucharistic worshippers?
• How do we make effective links between worship and mission?

Creative Communion offers valuable insights and resources to address these and other leading questions. It steers a helpful middle ground between providing food for thought on the one hand and offering tried-and-tested practical ideas on the other. It is a book whose wisdom will help churches get to grips with the challenge of celebrating dynamic, inclusive eucharistic worship.

As Margaret and Tim remind us, the Eucharist is about enabling us to experience and enjoy the presence of the living Christ, so that we may be transformed by the encounter. My hope and prayer is that *Creative Communion* may be well used to help churches grow in their understanding of the Eucharist as God's gift for all his people.

The Revd Peter Moger
National Worship Development Officer, The Church of England

⁜

Introduction

An encounter with the living God

It happened during a meeting of the worship committee. A group of church leaders was reviewing the Lent and Easter services and a lively conversation was taking place. Length of sermons, choice of hymns, the Palm Sunday procession, how the children had been involved, even the flowers in the Easter garden were discussed. Only the vicar remained silent. He sat with his head slightly bowed, listening carefully as each point was raised and taken apart. Eventually, Dora, the secretary, observed, 'You are being very quiet, Alex. What are you thinking?' Alex looked up. 'I think there are only two questions and we are in danger of missing them,' he replied. 'First, why are we doing this, and second, did each person present have an opportunity to worship and enjoy the presence of the living Christ?'

This book attempts to address these two questions by discovering creative ways in which people of all ages and stages of faith can meet and be touched by God through the service that Jesus himself left to his Church: the Eucharist or Holy Communion.

The last thirty years

The Church of England, as well as the other mainstream denominations, has been through 30 years of major liturgical change, before which the Book of Common Prayer of 1662 had remained supreme for three centuries. *The Alternative Service Book* (1980) was the first and biggest turning point, but the changes since then—the influence of the charismatic movement, new liturgies in other denominations and a response to various social and cultural changes—have been equally dramatic. In the last decade, the Revised Common Lectionary, various alternative texts and then *Common Worship* (2000) have broadened the use of scripture and allowed infinite variety to suit every situation. Word processing and desktop publishing have produced changes as radical as the invention of the printing press over 500 years ago.

Our duty and our joy

Liturgy, however, is more than words. In fact, the word means 'the work of the people', which shows us that fundamentally it is not about the given text. Because of the nature of the people and cultures in which we find ourselves, we now have a wonderfully rich diversity of resources to draw on, which are appropriate to our own situation. If liturgy is the work of the people, then worship is our primary calling and ultimate purpose. Whether we want to worship or not, this is how we have been designed as human beings. It can be expressed in one phrase from the Preface to the Eucharistic Prayer: 'it is our duty and our joy…' The sense of duty that used to take people to church is no longer enough. Worship is expected to be alive and relevant so that the worshipper has a sense of the presence of God and engages with him individually and as part of a Christian community. Therefore, Communion is not the work and sole domain of the priest, but of the whole priesthood of believers growing and journeying with God. The role of the priest or minister is to preside over this community celebration. Duty and joy go hand in hand.

Infinite variety

Today's liturgy can be seen as a framework rather than a straitjacket. Some parishes have been celebrating the Eucharist in an imaginative style, with special music, simplified texts and all-age groups fully involved, for two generations. The General Synod's decision in 1997 to allow children to receive Holy Communion before Confirmation in certain circumstances[1] encouraged many Anglican churches to re-evaluate their liturgy and try to see it through the eyes of a child, with the stress on the experience of the presence of God in his word and sacrament as much as on teaching about him. There are many other parishes, however, where the eucharistic worship has not been reviewed for at least 20 years and a few where the words and actions of the Book of Common Prayer remain unaltered.

A few churches still celebrate Holy Communion only as an early morning service for adult communicants. In many other churches it is the main service, but is designed as if only committed adult Christians are ever going to be present; children and occasional attenders are expected to join in as best they can.

A common pattern of such churches is to have a non-eucharistic service once a month, often called the 'Family Service'. These servies are often highly imaginative, with music, drama and visual aids designed to encourage active participation. This creativity does not always extend to the weekly Eucharist, however. It is often presented in a way that conceals the sense of the presence of God rather than revealing it, and does little to engage with a congregation of mixed ages and backgrounds.

Worshipping creatively

This book attempts to find ways of enabling the power of the Eucharist to speak to people of all ages and backgrounds more clearly, and to help us to work and worship creatively within whatever tradition or situation we find ourselves. It is in three sections:

✪ Part One looks briefly at the structure of the Eucharist and the various resources that can develop and enhance the worship. It also explores the opportunities and challenges of making the Eucharist a truly inclusive event, and the mission opportunities that can spring from it.

- Part Two is a series of six free-standing workshops, which explore different sections of the Eucharist creatively. Each one provides space for teaching, discussion and then a series of activities that can be included in future services or form the basis of occasional special services.
- Part Three ('Food, glorious food') is a programme intended for children and young people who have not yet been prepared for confirmation. Some of them may have been admitted to Holy Communion, while others will have attended the service on occasions. It is designed to help them to become familiar with the elements of the service, what it means in today's world and the practicalities of living out a Christian life at home, at school and with family and friends.

As the celebration of the Eucharist is the central act of worship for the majority of Christians, developing an understanding of it is an essential part of each person's spiritual journey. It is hoped that these programmes will help each person to worship as part of a community where all ages and stages of understanding are integrated and valued but also challenged and fed, whatever their age or spiritual experience.

Use of language

This book has been written principally from an Anglican perspective, but it is hoped that Christians in other denominations will find it of use in their exploration of any corporate worship including the service of Holy Communion. Most churches are moving closer together in their style of worship, with use of colour, music and signs and symbols that would have been unimaginable in some traditions

30 years ago. Misunderstanding often arises, however, from the terminology used, in that it is seen to be a sign of a particular tradition and thereby becomes exclusive.

The following glossary may be of use.

- **Altar:** Used generally, but some traditions prefer to use the term 'Communion table'.
- **Body of Christ:** The people of God, especially in the context of service.
- **Child:** Any person up to the age of about twelve years. 'Youngsters' or 'young people' implies a broader age span, maybe up to mid-teens.
- **Church:** When a capital 'C' is used, the word refers to the universal Church or a whole denomination, such as the Methodist Church. When lower case is used, it refers to the local church as a Christian community or a building.
- **Clergy:** An ordained person. 'Priest' or 'minister' is also used.
- **Congregation:** The lay people belonging to a church community.
- **Eucharist or eucharistic worship:** Eucharist means 'thanksgiving'. Along with Holy Communion, it is the name given to any service where bread and wine are blessed, broken and shared.
- **Liturgy and liturgical:** Any public service, especially in its design and delivery. It is not necessarily eucharistic, but covers any public act of worship.
- **President:** The person who has overall oversight of the worship. In Anglican churches, this is an ordained priest. In some other denominations there may be an appointed lay president.
- **Service:** More formal than 'act of worship'. For example, 'the main service is a Eucharist'; 'the meeting started with an act of worship'.
- **Worshipping community:** A slightly broader term than 'congregation', used largely in a pastoral context.

─────── Part One ───────

Living the story

The shape of
the Eucharist

'Hurry up, the meal is ready and on the table!'

Many families don't eat together much nowadays. Maybe you are part of a family in which eating and sitting together is an integral part of your day, but maybe it's just not possible, so using trays in front of the television or eating at different times is the only way you can make homelife work.

Nevertheless, eating together is important. Across most of the continent of Europe, time is 'squandered' in the day, eating and drinking and sharing as a family. As Christians, we need to reclaim the lost art of eating together and make it part of what it means to be growing up as a Christian. This lost art was often encapsulated in 'Sunday lunch', which was something of an institution for many families—and could be revived if the focus is around a Sunday morning Eucharist. We recognize, however, that there is an ever-increasing number of exciting ventures where churches are developing services of Holy Communion on different days and at different times. We are excited and affirmed by this new move of the Holy Spirit, but the most important thing is that we get together to eat. Let's do it on a day that is convenient for everyone!

The reason for this is that at the heart of our Christian faith is a meal. It can be a simple or elaborate celebration on any day of the week, but it is still a shared meal.

What follows is an elementary theology of the Eucharist, which we hope will be lived out through the workshops and sessions in this book so that Holy Communion with God in church will be food for our spiritual journeys—whatever our age or stage of faith. This chapter is designed to be used in a variety of ways: as a sermon to the whole church to explain the Eucharist to all ages or as a narrative to help work through the service.

'Oh, you can't do Holy Communion with children. It's too wordy, too long!'

This has often been said in countless churches, but we should refute it strongly. The Eucharist is a drama in which we are not only caught up but are also active participants. As baptized Christians, we all have an equal place at the table by the grace of God. Nothing is more important.

The Eucharist is a lived story. It is love in action, and it is a symbolic four-course meal for which we need to get ready.

Preparation: the gathering

There is nothing more frustrating than calling everyone to sit down at a meal table. Some come straight away and some delay. They are doing something, or outside, or on the phone, or just finishing a game on the PlayStation. We are reminded that we all come from different places, backgrounds and experiences when we sit around the table. We are not automata, programmed to sit at a particular time; nor are we institutionalized to do exactly the same thing at exactly the same time.

When we gather for Holy Communion, we need to recognize that we are all different. Therefore, care and attention need to be given to sharing what has been happening during the day, and preparing to eat. This can best be done by sharing stories of whether we have had good or bad days, or what has happened since we last met. It is an amazing thing to consider that every time we meet to eat together, we have become different people since the last time, because of the encounters we have had and the things we have learnt.

Confession as part of preparation

Part of the gathering is getting ready to eat, and a key part of this important routine is to wash our hands. Washing hands is about making ourselves clean to eat, preparing ourselves so that we can enjoy the meal together as much as possible. It is also about respecting the food we are going to eat, not wanting it to be spoilt by anything we might already have on our hands.

Washing hands is about saying sorry to God. This act of penitence is appropriate every time we gather to worship, and perhaps our churches need to provide opportunities for handwashing if they don't already do so. Saying sorry to God is the confessional rite of the church. In terms of the Eucharist, it is part of our preparation. Being absolved from our sins is as important as recognizing that we need to be physically clean before we eat.

Now we can celebrate! We sing (in the Eucharist, this is the place for the 'Gloria', which simply means 'songs of praise') of all that God is and what he has done for us, and we share his story and our story. This is what we do at the meal table. This storytelling is rooted in Jewish Passover tradition.

A four-course meal

The Eucharist is a four-course meal. The Eucharist meal has two substantial and equally important courses and two which, while not so substantial, are no less important to the whole.

The first course: The ministry of the word

The first course is when we feed on God's word together. (I often wonder whether we shouldn't put a knife and fork on the lectern as a sign that the Bible is food for us.) Care needs to be taken over how much of the Bible we read. Lectionary readings are often too long, which means we have so much on our plates that it's hard to digest or distinguish the different tastes.

We should also read the word carefully and find different ways of engaging with it. Many people, including children, learn most through doing and seeing, so visual ways of sharing the word need to be developed. After all, we don't sit down at a meal to learn how it was cooked, but to enjoy the food and to be nourished by it. In the same way, we don't come to church just to learn; we come to worship. So, while learning is vital, we learn through our worship as God reveals himself to us. In this book we have outlined a number of creative ways to help the whole worshipping community both to get a balanced diet and to consume it well.

The second course: the peace

The sharing of the peace is the pivotal point of the Eucharist. In the same way that we encounter the living Jesus in his word, we encounter the living God in each other. A former parish Reader's prayer went like this: 'I pray that today the little bit of God in me would recognize the little bit of God in everyone I meet, and that they would recognize the little bit of God in me.' It's simple, yet profound, and it goes to the heart of the peace.

This is the point in the Communion service where our focus shifts from one place—the encounter with Jesus in the word—to the altar and the bread and wine. Due care and attention need to be given to the sharing of the peace, to prevent it from turning into some sort of social interlude in the proceedings—a time when collection money is found or, worse, when the children are told to be quiet as they come into church. The peace is about sharing, so, if the children do come back into the church at this point, it is a good time to share what the young people have been doing, rather than leaving it to the end of the service. This is a good way to involve them as part of their sharing of the peace.

If we are to be a community of faith of all ages, the peace recognizes us as such. The sharing of the peace is the time when we truly offer our gifts and ourselves, and no offertory is complete without children as they are an integral part of the offering of the people of God. If the children are not gathered at this point, then the people of God are not complete.

The third course: the ministry of the sacrament

The ministry of the sacrament is the point where we gather and break bread. We share together in the same way that we have done through the other two courses, but we are also breaking open Jesus to share him. The priest or minister will stand with his or her hands outstretched, praying and inviting people to join in the feast. We can all join in this prayer; it is the big 'thank you' prayer of the church. Perhaps we could all put our hands out to pray, or all gather around the altar, or in other ways share in this prayer of thanksgiving for all that God has done for us.

It is worth saying here that many people struggle or have differing views over the presence of Jesus in the bread and wine—ranging from the belief that the bread and wine become the actual body and blood of Christ, through to the belief that they are just bread and wine. This is the question over the 'real presence of Jesus'. While wishing to respect individual convictions, for the purpose of this book it is important, whatever our view, to recognize that somehow Jesus is present. After all, we have never met anyone who has a doctrine of the 'real absence of Jesus'! As Richard Giles puts it in *How to be an Anglican*, 'The great thing about the sacraments is that Jesus always shows up!'[2] So let us rejoice in our diversity and celebrate the presence of Jesus in whatever way is comfortable and appropriate to us.

He is host, and guest, and the meal itself!

The fourth course: eat in or take away?

When I was young, I was taught to be polite and always say, 'Thank you for my tea. Please may I get down from the table?' I was usually requesting permission to leave so that the adults could get on with their talking, which was boring to me! But at the heart of the request was a plea to go.

The Catholic tradition of the church refers to Holy Communion as the 'Mass'. This word is rooted in the Latin *missa*: 'being sent'. We are the sent people of God and we have permission to go, but, because we are going from a table, we are full of that food. In Holy Communion, we take our food to feed a hungry and broken world. That is why the dismissal in the Eucharist is more than just permission to leave the table: it is permission to feed the world. It's not an escape clause; it's an engagement clause. To carry the food analogy further, we are an eat-in and a takeaway establishment! We are the carry-out bags that Christ uses to feed a hungry and needy world.

We need to explore in our worship how we can do that—not just gathering for food, but going to feed.

The Eucharist is a meal with four courses; a meal full of all the nourishment we need to live as Christians; a meal where we feast and celebrate the love of God who is present through the Bible, through each other and through bread and wine.

Welcome to the love feast!

Setting the scene of the Eucharist

In the first chapter, the Eucharist was described as being like a four-course meal. That leads us to ask about the setting, which makes every meal different, even if the food is the same. What makes each Eucharist respond to a particular situation, the type of congregation and even the building in which it takes place?

Even though we retain least by listening, more by seeing and most of all by doing, most of our worship is about listening to words, and sitting or standing still. We can worship God with our whole selves and this includes all of our senses: touch, smell and movement, as well as seeing and hearing. Many of our services take place in ancient buildings dedicated to the glory of God with music, stained glass and furnishings designed to give a sense of his presence and the beauty of holiness. They are wonderful aids to worship when used imaginatively. Modern churches and buildings such as school halls are flexible and give equal but different opportunities for creative and colourful worship, including music, drama, movement and visual aids.

The 'five balloons' syndrome

Before we explore the many creative ways in which we might approach eucharistic worship, we need to be aware that, in the desire to make Holy Communion (or any act of worship) exciting and appealing to children, there is often the danger of looking for gimmicks or multimedia extravaganzas—to make a 'sterile liturgy' more entertaining. More often than not, however, it is not the liturgy that is sterile, but the way it is done. People learn in different ways beyond the didactic, but if we dress up worship solely in order to make it exciting and appealing, the problem is that once people have enjoyed seeing five balloons, they will expect ten, then 15, then 20 and so on. After a little while, the shape of the Eucharist will have been hijacked by the need for the next exciting visual aid. We offer this warning only because we have been victims of it in the past. Holy Communion is not entertainment; it is an extraordinary feast of love given to us in bread and wine and the presence of Jesus. This is what excites us. Fun, joy and laughter are key ingredients in the recipe, but they are not the end meal.

With that in mind, let us now explore the many different ways in which our worship can be deepened.

Music

One of the strongest ways for people to express their corporate feeling is by singing together in one voice, where everyone can contribute, whatever their age or musical ability. Music expresses emotion more strongly than speech. It is abstract, having to be constantly recreated, and through our worship it can give us a glimpse of the presence of God. It is not surprising that many people will judge a service by its music. 'We sang my favourite carol' or 'I didn't know any of the hymns' will often be the first comment rather than anything about the preaching or the prayers.

This means that music can make or break a service, so we have to choose it carefully to make it an integral part of the liturgy. It is not about just picking a few hymns that go well; it means ensuring that the music enhances the service as a whole and thereby helps everyone to worship.

Music in the Eucharist comes under four headings:

- A free-standing hymn, song or psalm
- A setting of a text, for example, Gloria or Sanctus
- Music to accompany movement, such as a procession or during Holy Communion
- Music to set an atmosphere for worship: anthems and instrumental music, or music on CD

Choosing music for the different parts of the service leads us to ask:

- What style of music do we need at this point?
- How long should it last?
- What mood or text will enhance the theme of this service?

Once these questions are answered, there is a good chance that the music, however simple, will have a transforming effect on the worship and thereby feed the worshippers.

Hymns and worship songs

Hymns and psalms have been the mainstay of Anglican and Free church worship, but with the explosion of new music in the last 40 years there is now a huge variety of worship songs, ranging from hymns designed for unison singing with imaginative accompaniments to responsorial music, modern songs and simple chants.

Hymns and worship songs should be familiar so that everyone can join in. This does not mean reducing the choice to a few old favourites or the most banal. An all-age service lends itself to all-age music, which can vary from plainsong through various styles of hymns to a piece that was composed last week. Every taste and age can be included without having a mishmash of styles that grate on each other.

It is a good idea to find out what hymns and songs are sung in your local schools. Many children's hymns are suitable for all ages and give the children a chance to take a lead and teach the adults. New music can always be introduced as the congregation gathers about five minutes before the service. Both children and adults can quickly learn a strong tune, and a short rehearsal can be part of greeting the congregation and helping people to join in. Ending the rehearsal on a note of encouragement can lead into a time of positive silence before the service.

Settings and responses

There are now a large number of musical settings of the Eucharist as well as hymns and responsorial versions that are designed for congregational singing or give opportunities for a choir or small group to lead, with the congregation joining in the refrains. Responsorial psalms, Alleluias and chants, such as music from Taizé, provide simple and effective music with an opportunity for solo singers, choir and congregation all to have distinctive roles.

Instrumental music

Every act of worship needs space for contemplative prayer. Anthems or instrumental music to set the mood or to comment on some aspect of it can be offered by people with musical talents but prayed by everyone. Instrumental music can be played during the offertory or Communion. Many youngsters are skilled musicians and can enjoy contributing in this way. There is also an evangelistic angle, in that music may attract young people who have no other connection with the church.

Use what you have!

If your church has only a few resources, do not give up. Carefully chosen recorded music can be equally effective as background music. A melody can be played on a keyboard or even a recorder. It is also worth remembering that for a large part of the Church's history, people sang unaccompanied, and this can be the most effective music of all. Just sing!

Drama

As we read in the previous chapter, the Eucharist is a drama in which we are not only caught up but are also active participants. It is important, therefore, that any drama used within the service enhances the worship rather than detracting from it.

Using drama leads us to ask:

✪ Does this drama illustrate the Gospel or theme of the service?
✪ Will it engage with the various ages and stages of faith within the congregation?
✪ Will it provide food for thought so that each person can grow a little in his or her Christian life?

Whatever you plan, be realistic. Many church dramas are too long and complicated. Keep them short and simple. Also, avoid bringing children to the front of the church simply to act as 'performing monkeys'.

Seen and heard

Drama needs to be seen and heard. Use the building: walk up the nave and aisles; pretend that the pulpit is a boat or a place for angels; treat pews as entrance points, houses or even hills. Ensure that gestures are big and generous. If you don't have a sound system, keep speech to the minimum: use mime with a commentary, or have a series of tableaux.

Most children are used to speaking clearly in school, but a large building filled with strange adults can be terrifying, so many children (as well as adults) speak too fast and drop their voices at the end of sentences so that the sound gets lost. There is no easy answer to this. Practising in church with someone to set the pace, and projecting your voice towards a focal point, are helpful. The ideal way, however, is for the reader to be taped and to listen to him or herself. This takes time, but is useful if a person—for example, a Reader in training—is going to speak regularly.

Costumes and props

Drama also needs to be visually stimulating, so costumes and props can enrich drama. However, it is not necessary to have elaborate costumes and props. Modern dress is sometimes better than the inevitable paper wings and robes. Props can also be very simple.

Involving the congregation

The most important thing in drama is to engage with the congregation. There are several days during the Church's year when the whole congregation can actively take part in the drama. The Presentation of the Lord, often called 'Candlemas', which falls on 2 February, is an ancient and beautiful ceremony in which we process with candles in a darkened church to recall that Jesus is 'a light for all nations'. A Palm Sunday procession, starting a distance from the church to re-enact Jesus' entry into Jerusalem, gives everyone a chance to walk, shout and wave greenery. The Good Friday Passion can be read dramatically, with the whole congregation taking the part of the crowd.

Directing the drama

'Directing' is not as grand as it sounds. All that is needed is careful planning. Make sure that you know the script, that it will work in your particular building and that there are enough people available. Check that everyone will be available on the Sunday, preferably with a written reminder or, with children, a telephone call to the home. Sunday is a crowded day for many families and it is not unknown to find that a key character has not turned up because he is playing football or visiting his grandmother. This is even more important if the service is on another day or evening, as it may get overlooked under the pressure of school or Saturday activities.

Whatever you plan, see that you rehearse in the place where you are to perform, and that everything runs smoothly from the congregation's point of view. This is not just about ensuring that people can see and hear, but remembering that the drama is part of the ministry of the word. Be prepared to practise until a particular movement or line is correct. This will help the players to feel secure and relaxed on the day.

Good drama can add to any act of worship and is something in which everyone can take part, whatever their age or level of skill. Actions speak louder than words.

Movement

Actions not only speak louder than words, they are also vital ways of teaching and expressing ourselves in worship. Symbolic actions show meanings that cannot be articulated clearly in a few words, and are especially important in worship where there are people of every age and stage of understanding. In many churches, the practice of holding the Gospel book high in procession to the centre of the church illustrates vividly how Jesus is present among us in his word. Everyone, including a young child, can understand the mood of a person kneeling with a bowed head. Actions like this teach better than long explanations. They allow each person to take in at his or her own level and respond accordingly.

Posture and movement

Posture and movement remind us that we worship God with all of ourselves—which includes making ourselves part of the act of worship by looking and responding rather than kneeling with our heads in our hands and keeping silent. The various postures we use during worship demonstrate our relationship with God and each other. Standing together to sing demonstrates the unity of the people of God. Sitting is the most receptive position, so it is used for listening and learning. Kneeling, or sitting with head bowed, is a sign of penitence and humility. Processions for the Gospel or to the crib at Christmas, or for the whole congregation on occasions like Palm Sunday, add to the expression as well as the drama of worship.

Gesture

Gestures, such as using the sign of the cross or bowing at particular moments, describe emotion and reverence more strongly than any teaching. Offering a handshake at the peace is one of the simplest and most effective movements in the whole Eucharist, provided that it includes everyone. Newcomers can feel included even if the service is conducted in a foreign language if they receive a handshake and a smile. The priest's gestures are equally important: hands extended when saying 'The Lord be with you', and gestures made during the Eucharistic Prayer to illustrate the link between the prayer and the Last Supper, all speak clearly of the nature of God and his saving work among us.

Visual aids

Most worship takes place in a wonderful visual aid: the church building. This is often ignored or seen as a burden to maintain and keep warm and clean. Every church will have some if not all of the following visual aids:

✪ Furnishings, such as the altar or Communion table, font, cross, lectern and pulpit
✪ Lighting and candles
✪ Liturgical colours
✪ Pictures, statues and icons
✪ Stained glass

Using the building

The shape of the building and the placing of furniture are in themselves an aid to worship and teaching. Some churches are cruciform in shape. A font placed near the door gives a different message from one moved into the centre for a baptism. A Eucharist held with the seats in a circle around the altar gives a different message from one with chairs in rows some distance away, and so on.

Murals and stained glass taught the faith to generations of people who could not read. There is now a shift away from the book culture of the last century to visual effects through television, DVD and the Internet. We need to engage with today's culture in the same way, by using the illustrations around us as well as using pictures, icons and PowerPoint, and creating banners, frontals and displays. These could be based on the liturgical colours of the Christian year if this is appropriate to your tradition.

Furnishings and lighting

An open Bible placed in the centre of an altar or on a large lectern teaches about its importance. The Christmas crib, Easter garden, stations of the cross and prayer board all offer opportunities for worship and teaching.

Even the dullest of churches is improved by good lighting. New systems with dimmers make an enormous difference, even though they are expensive. A few carefully placed spotlights can add focus and depth at very little cost to aspects of the building that have been previously unnoticed.

A candle reminds us that Jesus described himself as the light for the world. Lighting a candle is increasingly being recognized as an aid to prayer as well as a recognition of an innate longing for God that cannot be put into words. The effect of flickering candles in a church is powerful and appeals to all generations. Candles are a silent witness that a place of worship is also a place of prayer, which is used by people at all times.

Visual impact

Every service has an immediate visual impact. The way that the people leading worship walk, stand and read says a lot about their attitude and commitment. Processions and movement need to be orderly; readers and intercessors should be in place and ready to read; musicians need to be attentive for the whole service, not just the musical bits. Robes and linen need to be clean and pressed and the altar area needs to be free from clutter. The priest or minister needs to be aware that he or she is always on view and is the focus of attention for much of the time. Some people, especially children, will always spot the slightest slips and be either amused or puzzled by them.

We often burden the liturgy with words and explanations when a simple image will convey the message so much more effectively. Visual images often last longest: children forming a tableau for a nativity play, a candlelit procession at dusk or a single figure kneeling before a large cross will stay in the mind long after the words are forgotten.

Involving children
in the Eucharist

Ever since a spring evening, near Jerusalem, when two grieving friends invited a stranger to join them for a meal and recognized the risen Christ, Holy Communion has been the distinctive form of worship for most Christians. Whether it takes place in a vast cathedral with heavily embroidered vestments and beautiful music or in a hut with a packing case for a table, the action is the same. Bread and wine are shared in response to the Lord's command, 'Do this in remembrance of me', and then the gathered community goes out into the world to witness to the gospel.

In the days of the early Church, Holy Communion was an intimate service reserved for committed Christians. For centuries in the Western Church, however, the whole community was expected to attend Mass every Sunday. It was part of their lives from babyhood and the faith was caught as much as taught. After the Reformation, the church and its services remained in the centre of the community, and the Sunday school movement of the 19th and first part of the 20th centuries ensured that most children received a basic Christian education, albeit separate from the church and its sacramental life. Today, only a minority of people attend any kind of church service regularly and numbers have been falling steadily. There is no longer any guarantee that today's parents know enough about the Christian faith to pass it on to their children.

But the tide is turning. There is a new awareness of children's innate spirituality and the importance of their experiencing worship. After decades of neglect and some hostility, there is a culture of openness and goodwill, with schools and children's organizations welcoming links with churches. Children of all ages are taking part in eucharistic worship in school as well as church; some receive Holy Communion and the numbers are increasing.

This raises a number of questions. For example, how do we involve children in eucharistic worship? How do we have a truly all-age celebration? How do we help everyone, whatever their age and stage of faith, to experience the presence of Jesus among us in his word and sacrament?

Involvement and engagement

A lot has been written and taught about making children feel welcome. One way is by giving them jobs so that they feel involved. These jobs may range from singing and serving, through taking part in the offertory and displaying work, to tasks like putting up the hymn numbers or working the sound system. Most youngsters enjoy these tasks and gain a sense of being valued through their contribution to the service. Then there are the very young children who cannot cope with a long service. Crèche areas and packs of books and toys are provided to occupy them; some have their own service books, and a few churches have a children's corner where the youngsters can have teaching that explores the readings in a way that is appropriate to their ages and stages of faith.

Although it is vital to welcome children of all ages by involving them and catering for particular needs, most of these excellent suggestions do little to involve children in the actual worship. They are only part of the picture. They contain the children but the children are, sometimes literally, placed around the edge of the service rather than being engaged in the heart of the worship.

The story of Jesus calling the first disciples—'Come with me, and I will teach you to catch people' (Matthew 4:18–22, GNB)—has a strong resonance of evangelism: making new disciples. Yet one of the most popular activities for teaching children about this passage is to make a net and decorate fish with the children's names on them to go in the net. The analogy of being kept safe in Jesus' net—his Church—is a strong one, but if you take the idea further, what happens to the fish? They have to stay in the net: they cannot move or develop, and eventually they will die and be eaten!

Much of our worship is about treating the children like fish in a keep-net. They are contained and entertained with no thought of engagement, let alone spiritual growth with a real experience of the presence of God that will disciple them.

The underlying attitude is that children are to be treated as passive beings, having worship done to them. Some children like to help and feel valued, but on its own this can be a substitute for true involvement. Youngsters often stay away from church on the weeks when they are not serving or doing another job because they know of no other way to engage with the worship.

Relationship

Children deserve the riches of the gospel. These riches need to be given to them appropriately, but children should not be expected to accept something shallow and superficial. An all-age Eucharist may be lively, but it should also nurture and challenge everyone. We need to ask whether the worship reaches out and engages with children and adults who have little knowledge of the Christian faith; whether it gives them an experience of the presence of God that will draw them to him. If it doesn't, it can be deeply excluding, the beauty and symbolism can be lost, children can feel that they are there on sufferance and visitors can feel bewildered.

A bishop once visited a church and said that he wanted to spend some time with the children during the service. He described it as an exercise in total exclusion. He had to leave the warm church during some lively music (either the first hymn or the *Gloria in Excelsis*) and walk through the rain to the church hall. After a lesson and activity, he then had to walk back to the church in silence and wait outside in the rain, getting wetter and wetter until a sidesman opened the door and said, 'You may come in now. We've finished Communion.' He joined the children as they crept up to the empty rail for a blessing, accompanied by the loudest sound on earth: 'Sshhh!'

Whether children are present for the whole service or have their own teaching is immaterial. Every situation is different and it is for each church to decide what pattern is best for the children and to review it regularly. If the children and adults spend the ministry of the word apart, however, it is not a case of letting *them* (the children) into *our* (the adults') service at the time that suits the adults, but of two parts of the community coming together, just as when the members of a family stop whatever different things they are doing to get around the table for a meal.

The Anglican tradition has been to organize worship as though only highly literate adults are going to be present and to expect everyone else to fit around the edge. If a Eucharist is to be truly all-age, it will include everyone, whatever their age or stage of faith. This involves planning and it often involves a change of thinking.

Planning

These comments are used all too frequently when planning a service that includes children.

- ✪ Let's get the children to do .... for us.
- ✪ That will keep them occupied.
- ✪ Do the sketch when flour is thrown... use the puppets... they'll like that.
- ✪ Get the youth club to act a play so that they feel they belong.
- ✪ The children were very good last time. [That is, they were quiet!]

Instead, plan the service by asking questions:

✪ How will we present the theme of this service with the wide age range present?

✪ What readings are we using? Are any adaptations necessary?

✪ How will music, drama or visual aids help everyone to worship with their whole selves?

✪ How will people of all ages be involved by being able to see, hear and respond?

✪ How will we give a sense of the presence of God with time and space for prayer?

Whatever the tradition, the Eucharist uses colour, light, music, movement and sometimes smell. It is a multifaceted and multi-sensory service that can include everyone if it is prepared carefully and creatively. It has so much to offer to children and that is why, when it is led with commitment and a sense of wonder, they can be caught up in it and experience a sense of the presence of God and of being part of a worshipping community.

One other factor outweighs everything else. Children will learn about the Eucharist through the colour, the music and the actions, but they will learn even more by the way their fellow Christians behave. They will learn more about what it means to be a Christian by the way the priest or minister presides at the Eucharist, and the way the adults worship and behave towards them and each other, than through the best teaching course in the world. The glare or the harsh word can be highly destructive, while to witness adults talking in the Communion queue or failing to join in the hymns and responses brings the dangerous negative message that worship does not matter and can be ignored.

Design and review

This leads us to the way in which an all-age Eucharist is designed. The Eucharist is easier than any other all-age service because the structure is there already. Everything is ordered; everyone has his or her assigned task; the words and movements are almost identical each time. The challenge of an all-age Eucharist is to provide something organic within this structure that develops and changes in response to the dynamic of the assembled people. A Eucharist in school on Friday afternoon, for example, is different from one on Sunday in church, which is, in its turn, different from one with a group of parents and youngsters on Tuesday morning.

The main changes in such a service are simple: they include the length and number of readings, prayers that are read and perhaps composed by children and adults, the use of the sound system, music that everyone can sing easily, service sheets in large print for youngsters as well as the elderly, and use of visual aids in teaching. Larger changes may involve moving the furniture, standing for prayers and receiving Holy Communion, or gathering the children around the altar for the Eucharistic Prayer. This can have an enormous impact on the children, and on the adults who see the concentration and sense of wonder on the children's faces.

High-quality worship requires work and constant review. A monthly all-age Eucharist may be very successful, but time and preparation need to go into every service to see that it is kept fresh and responds to the changing dynamics as children grow older, new families come, others leave, uniformed organizations attend or stay away, choirs grow and servers leave home. These changes all present challenges, and each service may have a different character from the last one.

Living the Eucharist

It is very easy to gather around the altar with our backs to the world. The Eucharist is about Jesus being risen and present among us, but it is also about betrayal, suffering and death. If it is to make sense, we have to live it in everything we do and to help children to live the Eucharist through our example as much as our teaching.

Listening carefully to God's word in the Bible should lead into our listening to children and helping them to listen to each other. Intercessions for the needs of the world, local issues, or those who are unwell or deprived need to be lived out through action. This can be through links with a mission agency or a charity, and by encouraging children to live out their prayers in their families and communities. Prayers for those who are unwell can be earthed by visiting a relation in hospital or making a card for a schoolfriend who is ill. Remembering refugees and people who are lonely can be put into practice by befriending a child who is new to the school or offering to walk home with someone who is alone.

Sharing the peace relates to dealing with a fight in the playground, learning not to bear a grudge, and basic courtesy to each other and to adults in authority.

Offering bread and wine relates to respecting the environment, valuing God's gifts to us and sharing them with people who are less well off. The dismissal is about living the Christian life. We go out as followers of Jesus Christ by witnessing in our schools, our homes, our workplace and with our family and friends.

It is not only possible, it is essential to involve everyone in the Eucharist, whatever their age or stage of faith. It is not just about including children; it is about giving everyone an equal status in the worship, as, indeed, they have in the eyes of God. A church that does the hard work and commits itself to providing worship where all ages are truly involved will find many rewards, not least in celebrating the vibrant faith and lively ministry of its youngest members.

Children receiving
Holy Communion

You are probably reading this book because you want to explore the whole subject of the Eucharist further. It may be because you feel that the service has become lacklustre and that there is room for more creativity. You may feel that the young people or the whole congregation need to be involved in reviewing the whole service and exploring how better to experience some of its richness and symbolism.

Whatever the reason, the subject of children and Holy Communion will come into discussion or into your own mind at some time. One of the many effects of all-age eucharistic worship in the early 1990s was that it made nonsense of the assumption that adults received Holy Communion and children did not. Leaders of uniformed organizations and occasional visitors came to the altar to receive a blessing while youngsters in their early teens who had been confirmed knelt beside them to receive Holy Communion. At the same time, the policy of welcoming communicant members of all Christian denominations and the increased number of immigrant families from parts of the Anglican Communion, where children were communicants from an early age, led to a small but significant number of children also receiving Holy Communion.

This brought to the forefront the question of whether children should be allowed to receive Holy Communion, which had been simmering in the background for nearly 30 years. Reports had been written and pilot schemes had been set up in three dioceses, and the climate for inclusiveness was growing. Even so, Stephen Lake wrote, when recalling the all-age eucharistic services that he held in his church in Branksome, 'Discrimination was alive and well, in the church and in my parish and at the altar!'[3] For him, as well as countless others, their church appeared to be an all-age worshipping community but lacked the most important and defining characteristic. It was denying the sacrament to baptized and practising Christians solely on grounds of age.

In 1997, the General Synod eventually gave permission for children to be admitted to Holy Communion before confirmation under certain circumstances and with the diocesan bishop's permission. Far from the predicted explosion of demands and chaos, progress has been slow and steady. Some parishes welcomed the change with open arms; others discussed it carefully and over a period of time. By July 2005, when the General Synod reviewed the practice, about eleven per cent of parishes were admitting children, from a total of 39 out of 43 dioceses. The more striking change was in Church schools, where eucharistic worship was becoming more common, with about 50 per cent of schools having it at some time. Increasingly, some schools are becoming eucharistic communities, based on a life of prayer, with children and occasionally staff and parents being baptized, admitted to Holy Communion and confirmed. There is, however, a long way to go before this practice becomes common, let alone the norm.

The number-crunching statistics of the report under discussion gained vitality at the Synod debate as person after person spoke about how children receiving Holy Communion had transformed and enriched their churches, and how whole families had become more committed, with a positive effect on the worshipping community. The children's faith and reverence, with their enthusiasm for the things of God, had changed people's hearts and minds. If your church welcomes children to receive Holy Communion, you will probably find that you, too, are celebrating the way that this has enriched your parish's life in the last few years. But we hope that you will not leave it there. Admitting children to Holy Communion is the beginning of the story, not the end, and any church will need constantly to review its nurture and worship for people of all ages, to ensure that it keeps its vitality and reaches to all generations and stages of faith.

It is beyond the scope of this book to discuss ways in which churches that have not admitted children can explore the subject. Stephen Lake gives an outline of the history and various reports,[4] and the practicalities for a church considering moving forward are found in the first part of *Welcome to the Lord's Table*.[5] Whatever procedures are in place, however, it is vital that the whole worshipping community explores the Eucharist as part of its discussion and planning. This can happen through preaching and teaching but more effectively by active exploration and discussion. Part of that process could be that the parish explores the Eucharist through all-age workshops, such as the programme of workshops in Part Two of this book (see 'Exploring the Eucharist in all-age workshops' on page 47). Working through the all-age workshops will almost certainly raise the subject of why there is discrimination when children approach the altar, even when they are involved in the service.

Admitting children to Holy Communion affects everything that a church does: education, finance and social life—even the way buildings are used—are viewed from a slightly different perspective. Most of all, however, the worship has to take into account the place of children around the Lord's table. This involves more than practicalities; it is about including people of all ages in a service that has been designed solely for adults. Much of this has already been discussed in the earlier chapters of this book, and churches with experience of all-age eucharistic worship will probably find the progression straightforward. Such services do not have to be geared towards the lowest common denominator but can genuinely reach to all ages and stages of faith. Above all, it affects us because we grow in fellowship and discipleship as the whole people of God are brought into a transforming encounter with God. Communion is meant to change us more into the likeness of God.

Use of sign, symbol, music and drama can make the worship accessible while retaining a challenge to the intellect and spirituality of everyone. We all learn as much from signs and symbols as from words, and the ceremonial at the Eucharist can be unfolded as a teaching aid in itself. Most young children are naturally reverent, so it is a case of helping them to apply that reverence to the holy gifts given to God's people in his word and sacrament. Eucharistic devotion and understanding will not trickle down automatically through the generations to the youngest children. We must be immersed in it together as the people of God. With sensitivity and planning, all can feel included and feel a sense of the presence of God.

Evangelism and Communion for young people

What is evangelism?

The word 'evangelism' still strikes fear into many people. With children there is even more nervousness. Are we coercing children or brainwashing them at a young age? Not so! Let us clear up some myths before offering some simple truths and suggestions for evangelism.

Evangelism is not about standing on street corners, heckling passers-by with a floppy Bible the size of a tennis court and a megaphone on full distorted volume. This sort of activity does evangelism a disservice. At its heart, evangelism is simply sharing good news and passing good news on. This is a basic human instinct and deep within the nature of children. They can't wait to tell us things—how they got on at school, a prize they won, a goal scored, a new friend made. Evangelism is about sharing good news of what Jesus means to us. As adults, we have become inhibited and diffident when talking about faith, seeing it as a private matter rather than something of public concern. Yet, in the Gospels, there is no such thing as a private faith: that idea runs counter to the Bible. We do have a personal faith, but that is different from being private. Part of the process of evangelism is getting used to sharing good news about God and the church and about our feelings. Without this sort of communication, we cannot make Jesus known. Increasingly, we need to be more explicit about our faith, without being afraid.

Children are often the best evangelists because they don't have the inhibitions and hang-ups that accrue with age. As we have already said, children make connections less with words and more through visual, sensory and kinaesthetic activity. In other words, if you want children to be captured by something, make it visual, engaging and practical.

In the story of the appearance of Jesus to the disciples on the road to Emmaus (Luke 24:13–35), Jesus draws alongside two disciples. The dialogue is in many ways childlike: it is full of questions and full of answers and stories. These stories make the hearts of the disciples 'burn' (v. 32). They are not being taught; rather, it is the relationship that develops in those seven short miles that makes such a difference. It is a story of word and sacrament, and it is a relationship that culminates in the recognition of Jesus in the breaking of the bread.

Evangelism is about relationships

Relationships matter to everyone, but they matter deeply to children. Children will offer great trust when time, care and love are invested in them. You only have to watch a child who has been lost, or away from a parent for a period of time, as they run to greet the parent, to see an icon of total trust. The material in this book (and in *Welcome to the Lord's Table*) is primarily about developing an ongoing relationship—a pilgrimage, almost—with the children entrusted to our care. On the Emmaus road, Jesus and the disciples committed themselves to an accompanied journey on which Jesus would have gone as far as necessary in order for the disciples to recognize him, but without the faintest whiff of the coercion we often associate with evangelism. We should be intentional in our relationships, but never manipulative with children—always waiting for them to prompt us and responding to them.

Evangelism is about excitement

On the road to Emmaus, the hearts of the disciples 'burned within them' (v. 32). Nowadays, we might say that the hairs on the back of their necks were standing up, or that they were jumping up and down with a growing excitement. Integrating children is not about making sure they come to church or that they keep our own grown-up show on the road. It is about helping them to feel full members of the worshipping body of Christ, which includes taking the risk that they will bring their unbridled joy and excitement to the table—not to have that joy diffused, but so that it may overflow into the rest of the community.

Evangelism is about the Holy Spirit

Evangelism is not about our works but about the work of God in the lives of children. Our work in presenting this material and this meal and helping it come alive is simply to be an enabler of the Holy Spirit, to help the children to recognize Jesus. Any meal can look great in the recipe book and even good on the plate, but unless those words 'Yum, this is nice' are uttered from the mouth of the child, then all our labours have been in vain. The tasting and the recognition are the work of God: our work is to be the preparers and co-workers in the process of this most basic, yet most profound, feast of love. We should never think that our own efforts or the material we use is the most important thing. We should pray, and mobilize our churches to pray, not just for the people doing the necessary work, but that the Holy Spirit would break through as he did for the disciples, so that they would recognize Jesus.

Evangelism is about recognition, not total understanding

We don't need to understand everything about God or, indeed, work through a contrived syllabus to the point of becoming a Christian.

The process may take weeks, it may take years, but each contribution is a small drop in the ocean of the process. All of what we do with children is to help them recognize Jesus, and this will not always be an intellectual process. Of course, children think deeply, but they also feel deeply and they think and process information with their eyes and their hands.

Evangelism is about moving from receiving to sharing

In a short chapter on children and evangelism, it is easy to assume that it's all about how we can evangelize children. It is not! It is also about how children can evangelize the church. Children are often the most effective evangelists in sharing the good news and revealing things to us grown-ups that we have missed. Many people's understanding of the faith has been helped through seeing the willingness of children to offer themselves unconditionally; children often receive the bread and wine as something special, in a way that paints a picture for the rest of the church of how to approach Holy Communion.

Evangelism is not noisy but silent

Another caricature of evangelism is that it is noisy, emotive and emotional—that it manipulates people and therefore lacks integrity. The story of the recognition of Jesus at Emmaus, by contrast, is about the quiet whisper and dialogue of Jesus with these two disciples, and the sheer normality of an evening meal with an unexpected guest. Therefore, while a stimulating, lively and noisy Communion can be relevant and completely appropriate on occasion, sometimes a still, quiet and atmospheric service will be one where Jesus speaks into the hearts of children and adults alike.

None of the advice in this chapter is necessarily unique to children, since Communion is a meal for all the family to share from an early age. None of us can fully understand the mystery of Christ made present in Communion, but none of us advocates any theology of the absence of Jesus in Communion. He is indeed there. Evangelism is about helping children to recognize for themselves—like those first disciples at Emmaus—Jesus made present in the breaking of the bread.

—— Part Two ——

Exploring the Eucharist
in all-age workshops

✣

Before you begin

This programme is a series of free-standing workshops that offer practical ways to reflect on and creatively explore the Eucharist, in order to bring a new imaginative dimension to the liturgy. Each workshop is designed so that people of all ages, including children, can take part, but it could also be used by a designated group such as the church council, a worship committee, a group of young people or even the whole church.

Aims of the workshops

✪ To reflect on the meaning behind each section of the Eucharist.
✪ To explore each section creatively through the Bible, music, craft and other activities.
✪ To find ways to enhance eucharistic services and other special services through what has been learnt.

Learning styles

The style of teaching in these workshops is a mixture of formal and 'hands-on'. The Bible passage and teaching at the beginning of each session are intended to set the scene and provide some straight-forward insights. The activities that follow complement and develop the session in a practical way.

Most teaching in church is didactic and assumes that the people taking part are familiar with the Bible, knowledgeable about the Christian faith and able to articulate it. However, because we know that we learn and remember most through what we see and do rather than what we hear, the activities are deliberately designed to use craft, drama and movement, as well as including music as part of the programme. Most people enjoy the opportunity to do something practical and this gives a chance for the less articulate to express their faith in other ways.

The group

The outline of each programme is a guideline, and the way it is used will depend on the size and composition of your group. If the group is small and comprises mainly adults, the discussion and teaching may take a shorter time than suggested. If the group is large, it would be advisable to allow more time and to consider dividing into smaller groups for feedback and reflection. It is vital that children, if present, are fully involved throughout. They should contribute to any discussion and the leader should ensure that they are given an opportunity to do so. If there are large numbers and several groups but only a few children, it may be advisable to put the children together rather than spreading them too thinly among the adults.

The programme

Each workshop is designed to last about two and a half hours, so Saturday morning or possibly Saturday or Sunday afternoon are the best times, although an evening meeting is possible. The workshops can be spread over a longer period, such as a church's awayday, by allowing more time for discussion, a larger variety of activities and a fuller act of worship at the end. This could be based on the section of the Communion service being discussed that day—an extended penitential rite, time of creative intercession, and so on—or could be a full service of Holy Communion incorporating what has been learnt.

An approximate timetable for a two-and-a-half-hour session would be:

1. Icebreaker and welcome	20 minutes
2. Song	10 minutes
3. Teaching and discussion	25 minutes
4. Refreshment break	15 minutes
5. Activities	45 minutes
6. Reflection	20 minutes
7. Further action and planning	10 minutes
8. Notices	5 minutes

Keep a firm eye on the time and allow a few minutes for packing up or moving to the next part of the session. Don't let one part run on too long at the expense of another. Aim to end the discussion a few minutes before the finishing time to allow time for notices and information about the next session.

As each session demands a certain amount of preparation and follow-up, we do not recommend holding the workshops on consecutive weeks. Eucharistic worship is a huge subject and it is worth taking time to explore each section and reflect upon it. Moreover, if the aim is to make the ongoing eucharistic worship more imaginative and creative, it will take time for each innovation to be prepared, accepted and incorporated.

Venues

The obvious place in which to meet is the church hall, if you have one, or the church building. Few church buildings are ideal for this sort of session, but, as it is the place where the service is usually held, it could be easier to think through the present practice and visualize possible developments in situ. Meeting in the church building also has the advantage of enabling you to put any craftwork into place immediately.

Another option, if you can afford it, is the local school or a conference centre. These have the advantages of being warm, with good toilet facilities, several rooms and furniture that can be moved easily. If possible, arrange an area with comfortable chairs for discussion and teaching and put the various activities in other parts of the building.

Wherever the workshops are held, remember to tell people where the various facilities are and allow time for them to move from one activity to another. This can take as much as five minutes with a large group or if elderly or very young people are present.

Preparation

Good preparation is vital. Even if you are an experienced leader or teacher, read through the programme and spend some time on the aims and outcomes so that you know what the learning objectives are. Think about the section of the service that is being explored and the meaning behind it. Read the relevant biblical passage and teaching, which provide the basis for the discussion and activities that follow.

Prepare the meeting place in advance. Think about the arrangement of chairs, remembering that a large group may need to divide into smaller groups, but that people should be able to see each other's faces. When working as a whole group, a circle or horseshoe is usually best.

As many of the activities are craft-based, you will need to collect materials. This takes time! Paper and card can be bought cheaply from wholesalers. 'Pound shops' sell packs of pens. If you need 'junk', such as cardboard tubes from kitchen rolls, jam jars or textiles, ask the congregation to help and have a crate available at the back of the church for contributions. Each activity needs someone to lead it, but it is not necessary for leaders to be particularly skilled, provided the equipment is there. Give each activity leader an opportunity to see what is needed and to organize his or her area before the session starts.

See that you arrive early so that everything is prepared and you can greet others as they arrive.

Leading teaching and discussion

✪ At the first session, invite people to introduce themselves to each other. The icebreaker may provide this opportunity.

✪ Try to include everyone in discussion by encouraging a quiet person to contribute. Ensure that children are kept involved. As they are used to formal class discussion, they may be unwilling to join in without being invited. Be firm but polite with the person who is inclined to take over, by identifying and inviting other people to speak first.

✪ Do not assume that people who are involved with leading worship—Readers, servers, musicians and so on—are necessarily the experts. Everyone contributes to the worship by being present and the perspective from sitting in the congregation or being a young child often contributes something that those at the front have missed.

✪ Do not talk too much yourself. Allow time for silence and thought. If discussion seems to be getting nowhere, draw together the subjects that have been raised, then ask if there is anything else to be added.

✪ Conclude the discussion by explaining about the rest of the programme before the refreshment break. This helps the session to progress smoothly without breaks for information.

Using the Bible

In any Bible study group, there will usually be nearly as many versions of the Bible used as people reading it. In a programme of this type, it is important that the version used communicates with everyone present, whatever their age or level of literacy. It is worth looking at several versions carefully, bearing in mind the needs of the group.

The edition used in this book is the Contemporary English Version. We also recommend the New Revised Standard Version, the Good News Bible and the New International Version, particularly if any of these is the Bible generally used by the church. Versions for children and young people include the New International Revised Children's Bible (Zonder Kidz) and the *Barnabas Children's Bible* (Barnabas), which is a retelling of 365 Bible stories for children aged seven and above. For young people, you might wish to consider *The Word on the Street* (Robert Lacey, Zondervan, 2005) and *THE MESSAGE* by Eugene Peterson, both of which also retell the story in modern language. Whichever translation you choose, try to ensure that it uses gender-inclusive language.

Music

The hymn or song for the session can be taught and sung at the beginning as part of setting the scene and drawing the group together, or as part of the reflection time and act of worship. It can also be included when planning a service. Most hymn and song books contain thematic and biblical indices.

In addition, quiet recorded music is useful for gathering people before the time of reflection and setting a calm atmosphere after an active time.

The activities

These are practical ways of exploring and enhancing each part of the service. They are designed so that everyone, whatever their age or stage of faith, can join in and learn in their own way. Indeed, some people who are used to leading and speaking will find themselves being helped with craft activities by people, including children, who are used to using their hands. Others will find that they have gifts and skills to offer that have hitherto remained hidden.

Reflection and prayer

This short time is for speaking briefly on what each person has gained by taking part and then summing it up in a short act of worship. A song may be sung here as part of the time of prayer. However it is done, it is important that time and space are given to reflect and offer the workshop to God.

Follow-up

Unless the workshop forms part of a whole day, there will not be time for detailed follow-up as part of the session. Use the 'Getting ready for Sunday' time to decide what to do with any crafts and to identify which other activities the group wants to include in a future service. Arrange for a small number of people to take responsibility for carrying this out, using the 'Making Sunday special' instructions at the end of each activity for guidance.

Decorative work can be put in the church immediately, but it is wiser to leave anything but the simplest activities until the next week at the earliest, so that there is time to improve on any rough work, include information in the notice sheet and incorporate the activity into the worship. The last will probably include briefing people and, maybe, a short rehearsal.

Arrange for a review of how the session went afterwards, either before the next workshop or by seeking feedback from the congregation as a whole. Take special note of any positive suggestions or things that could be done better in future.

Focus and select

We hope that exploring the Eucharist in a creative way will lead to a greater insight and enthusiasm for Communion, and that it will develop an understanding of the many ways in which the words of the Eucharist can be enriched by activity and participation, and help to lead us into a deeper awareness of the presence of God.

When a particular theme is being emphasized through the readings and the preaching, focus on it through the liturgy, too. The choice of hymns and songs to reflect the subjects as well as the parts of the service is important. Using some of the activities in this programme during different seasons and occasions will add a similar focus. During Lent, you may want to have an extended penitential rite, using the forgiveness tree (see pages 67–68), and balance it by omitting a reading or a hymn. You may want to emphasize the gathering and going out with special decorations and activities when the theme is about mission. Texts like the *Gloria* can be replaced with simpler versions when there are a large number of children or visitors present.

However, be aware that there is a danger of being carried away by enthusiasm and trying to focus on too much. This can result in a service that is far too long and a hotchpotch of ideas with no particular focus. Creativity in worship is like salt or spices in cooking. Too much can mask the basic flavours and even make the food unpalatable, whereas a little, used carefully, can transform a dish. Careful planning will ensure a right balance. Your service does not have to include every idea (there is always next year) but, over the months, you should include everyone, enhance the worship and give food for thought. There must be mutual tolerance in the family of the church as in any other family, to allow learning and understanding to develop.

Gathering

Pull yourself together!

Aim
To show that when we come together for worship, we recognize that we are all different but all have something to offer. We are the family of God. Each one of us is an individual but joined as part of that family.

Outline and suggested timing
See page 50 for information.

Icebreaker

Offer one of the following activities as people assemble.

Badgered!

You will need: a few mirrors, either on the walls and tables, or mirror tiles, blank card badges (the larger the better), felt-tipped pens and crayons.

Badge templates can be bought or made easily by drawing and cutting out circles and then fixing safety pins to the backs with sticky tape. If you can hire a badge-making machine, that is even better. Your diocesan education office or local school may have one that can be hired or borrowed.

We are all different! Invite people to look into a mirror and then draw a portrait of themselves on the badge. If you have the resources and time, you could do this on T-shirts instead.

Talent wall

You will need: several large sheets of paper attached to the wall or a display board, and large felt-tipped pens.

Invite people to write their name along with something new or different that they have done this week, no matter how big or small—for example, bought a new pair of shoes, passed a spelling test, been to a place not visited before, learnt a new skill, helped someone in need and so on.

When everyone has finished, gather them together. Make the point that while we are all different, we are all part of the family of the Church. Today is all about gathering and coming together. Invite everyone to look at the person sitting next to them. Ask, 'How are they different from you? Do you think that God values or loves them any more or less than he values you?' Explain that the answer is 'No!' He welcomes and values everyone just the same. When we meet for worship, we are all different, rather as the individual members of any family are different. Family gatherings are important because, although we have different lifestyles and interests, we are joined together by a common bond. Granny might well be oblivious to what an iPod is, while young children might be bewildered by talk of the British Empire. The point is that we are all related. We might not get on that well with the cousins, but they are still part of our family, so we make an effort not just to get together but also to get on together.

The Christian family is no different. We are joined by a common shared knowledge of God and a desire and need to meet together to worship. So how do we express this in terms of gathering around the Lord's table, and how do we welcome one another?

The aim of this session is to review the way that we gather as God's family at the Eucharist and to find out if there are ways in which we can do this more imaginatively.

Song

As we are gathered (MP 38)
Heaven invites you to a party (TS 150)
Here in this place (CHE 253)
One shall tell another (MP 541)

Teaching and discussion

Read Luke 7:12–23. This is a story of a great feast. Who is invited to the party? Ask everyone to think of a special party that they have been to. What sort of party was it? Why was it so special? What do they remember about it?

What about a party that they or their family gave for a birthday, the New Year and so on? Who did they invite? What did they do at the party?

Who didn't they invite? Was there any reason why they didn't invite some people? (Some of the answers here will be about only having space for a certain number of people at the party, and some will be about people they chose not to invite.)

Key teaching point

If Jesus held a big celebration, who do you think he would invite? In a service of Holy Communion, Jesus is inviting us to a very special party. Just because it happens more often than a birthday party, that doesn't make it any less special. When Jesus invites us, he invites everyone to gather and everyone is welcome. Can people think of anyone they don't get on with or don't know very well, who they might want to invite to Jesus' party?

Take a short break for refreshments at this point.

Activities

All or some of these activities can be set up around the church or hall so that everyone can choose to do one or two of them as time permits.

Elijah chair

You will need: four kitchen roll tubes, a piece of mediumweight A4 card, paint, brushes, PVA or sticky tape. Cloths and newspaper are also useful.

In the Jewish tradition, many houses have what is called an 'Elijah chair'. On special occasions, the family will set the table for one more person than they know is coming and will cook enough food for one more person. They do this as a reminder of unexpected guests and people who are not present but always welcome at the Lord's table.

Bend the card into an L shape two-thirds of the way down the length, to make the back and seat of a chair. Cut two kitchen roll tubes down to size to make two more L shapes for the arms. Stick one end of each arm to the back and the other end to the seat of the chair. This will keep the seat and back in a firm L shape. To complete the chair, add legs made from the other two kitchen roll tubes, cut in half and secured by tape at the four corners of the seat. The chair is, of course, just a model and not intended to be sat on! Paint the chair in bright colours or to look like wood.

Making Sunday special

Place one of the model chairs at the front of the church near the altar as a reminder of people who we would like to be at the service. On Sunday, you could stick Post-it notes on the chair, showing people or groups of people who are not represented in your church—for example, those caught in the poverty trap, those who cannot travel to church, people who are frightened to go out and so on.

Belonging and serving

> **You will need:** a large piece of plain cloth or strong paper cut to the size of an altar frontal, mediumweight card, scissors, felt-tipped pens and crayons, glitter glue and a picture or outline of your church building.

Invite each person to draw around his or her hand, colour and decorate the outline as they wish and add their name. Stick the picture of the church in the centre of the frontal. Cut out and stick each hand on to the frontal around the shape of the church so that they are fanned out attractively.

 Making Sunday special

Attach the frontal to the front of the altar, either by stapling the cloth around a long pole or by using masking tape. If this is not possible or your church does not use frontals, display it in a place where everyone can see it as they enter the church.

Thumbs up for the cross

> **You will need**: a piece of heavyweight card with a large template of a cross drawn on to it, a selection of coloured ink pads (don't just use black!), some damp cloths and soap and towels, or baby wipes.

Everyone's fingerprint is unique to him or her. Invite each person to roll their thumb along an inkpad and put their thumbprint on to the cross.

Making Sunday Special

Fix your cross template to the crucifix or cross that is used in the procession on Sunday (if you use one), or to any large cross in the building.

Paper chain

> **You will need**: strips of paper cut out of pieces of coloured paper to make paper chains (approximately 15cm x 3cm), and a stapler.

Invite each person to write his or her name and something about themselves on a strip of paper and join it in a loop to another strip to form a chain. The completed chain can be hung around the door during the workshop.

Making Sunday special

Take up the chain as part of the opening hymn in church and place it around the altar for the whole service. In order to include people who have not been at the workshop, you could invite people to add their own piece of chain when they arrive in church on Sunday.

Living stones

> **You will need:** a large sheet of paper or card showing an outline of your church building, pinned to a display board, adhesive labels and felt-tipped pens.

1 Peter 2:5 says, 'And now you are living stones that are being used to build a spiritual house.' This activity shows that we are all living stones building up the church. Each one of us has a part to play and each one of us is different.

Invite each person to write his or her name on a label and decorate it. The decoration could include something about the person's talents and interests. Stick the labels as bricks on to the outline of the church. As this activity is about making a building that holds together, encourage people to start at the bottom and gradually build the walls rather than placing the bricks at random.

A further teaching point would be to place twelve large stones along the bottom of the church to show that it is built on the teaching of the apostles, the first Christian leaders.

If you really want to think big, you can make a 3D version with shoeboxes. Cover a side of each shoebox in plain paper, then write names on them and design them as above. The boxes can be built into a 'Jenga church'.

 Making Sunday special

Display your 'living stones' wall in church. As with the previous activity, you could invite people to add labels with their names to the building at any time.

Reflection and prayer

As people gather after the activities, play some quiet music to calm the atmosphere. Ask if anyone would like to share his or her thoughts on:

❂ what we have experienced through doing the activities.
❂ anything else that could be included during a Sunday Eucharist or another service.
❂ anything we can do to make visitors more welcome.

Light a candle and place it in the centre of the group. You might want to put some background music on or have a short silence to create a quiet atmosphere.

Loving God, thank you that you invite us to your party every time. Thank you for the different people in the Christian family. Forgive us when we don't get on with others or they find it hard to get on with us. Help us to realize that we are one family joined by you. We gather here to say we love you, Lord. Amen

Further action and planning

This should take into account the answers to the second bullet point in the Reflection. Also include the 'Making Sunday special' suggestions from each of the activities. Discuss briefly which of the activities will be used in a future service and arrange for a group of people to meet to implement the suggestions.

Adults and older children might like to look at the church and see how it could change to be more welcoming, especially for those who have special needs or disabilities, or for babies. How could you make your church building more welcoming and an easier place for everyone to gather? What improvements could be made to increase the sense of welcome from you, the gathered people?

Penitence

Wash your hands first!

Aim

To reflect on how we are made in God's image, but sometimes spoil that image by getting things wrong and not being the whole people that he wants us to be. Before we meet God in Holy Communion, we need to think about the things we have done wrong—called sin—and receive God's forgiveness.

Outline and suggested timing

See page 50 for information.

Icebreaker

Distorted reflections

This exercise follows the icebreaker in the previous workshop, about looking into mirrors. Collect some ceramic tiles, polished metal or glass that will only show a poor reflection. If you can find some items that give a distortion in the way of the mirrors found at funfairs, so much the better. Ensure that everyone has a pen and some paper to write on.

Invite everyone to take a reflective item and look at their reflection. Can they see themselves clearly? Does their face look a different colour? Is there any distortion? Can they see all or only part of their face?

Ask everyone to write down how they look. Do they prefer themselves like that or as they really are?

Invite everyone to think about something in the world that is wrong. This may be something they have seen on the news or it may have happened locally. After a pause, ask everyone to think about something they have done that was wrong. This may have been an accident, something that they forgot to do, or something they did deliberately. These things spoil our relationship with God and each other, just as the reflections of ourselves in the distorted mirrors are spoiled.

Song

Bless the Lord, my soul (Taizé) (CHE 81)
God forgave my sin in Jesus' name (MP 181)
Just as I am, without one plea (MP 396)
Water of life, cleanse and refresh us (CHE 401)

Teaching and discussion

Read Matthew 5:21–26. In this story, Jesus is teaching about being reconciled (or becoming friends again) with people we have offended or hurt. We cannot take away the hurt but we can show we are sorry and do what we can to put it right.

Ask what can be done to put things right. Answers will include apologizing by saying 'sorry' to the person we have harmed, and trying to do better. This is often very difficult. Stealing can be dealt with by giving money to charity; sums missed out on a tax return can be added in the next year. We can make an effort to be pleasant to someone we dislike, and so on. You will find that children often have a clearer idea of right and wrong than adults, but you may have to explain that two wrongs do not make a right (as in 'he hit me first').

Key teaching point

Before we receive Holy Communion, we need to call to mind the things we have done that have distorted our lives and spoiled our friendship with God and each other. Owning up to them is rather like washing our hands before a meal. This is part of getting ready to meet Jesus in his word and sacrament.

Take a short break for refreshments at this point.

Activities

Choose from the following activities according to the composition of the group and the time available. There should be time for everyone to do a practical and a very short activity.

The forgiveness tree

The aim of this activity is to help the participants to reflect on the many aspects of sin: personal wrongdoing, society's failings and the injustices in the world order. It demonstrates that when we hear the words of God's forgiveness, we can be transformed through his grace and new life is made possible.

You will need: a bare branch or bundle of long twigs stuck into a pot of earth to be a 'tree', brown paper, tissue paper, glue sticks, scissors and pens or pencils.

Using brown paper, make plenty of leaves that are big enough to write on. Make a similar number of flowers out of brightly coloured tissue paper. You will need two or three of each for each person present.

Ask each person to think about the sins that they can identify (personal wrongdoings or the failings of the world) and write one on each brown paper leaf. Have two or three helpers ready to fasten the leaves very lightly to the branches of the 'tree' with touches of a glue stick.

Say together a prayer of confession or penitential rite. When the priest says a prayer for forgiveness, the helpers shake the branch until all the leaves have fallen off. Play some simple music. The helpers then decorate the tree with the flowers as a visual sign of the new life brought through receiving God's forgiveness. Alternatively, if the group is small, everyone can come forward to put a flower on the tree while some simple music is played.

Making Sunday special

This activity can form an extended penitential rite during the Eucharist or could be a short service on its own. Give each person a paper leaf and a pen or pencil as they enter the church and ask them to think about and then write on the leaf any wrongdoings of their own or failings of the world that come to mind before the service. Make sure there are adults available to help unescorted children.

After a brief introduction and explanation, have a moment of reflection and then indicate that people should put their leaves on the tree. (**NB:** they have to be stuck very lightly so they can be shaken off easily.) The flowers can be added after the prayer for forgiveness or after the Gospel reading.

If the rite is being used as part of a freestanding service such as a reconciliation service or a children's Holy Week club, the flowers and leaves can be made as part of the preparation for the service.

Nail it (or staple it)

You will need: a wooden cross made from two pieces of wood at least 5cm thick, some hammers and 3cm nails (fabric and staplers for younger children), 'U-turn' arrows on red card and 'forgiveness' arrows on white card (see pages 162 and 163 for templates).

NB: This activity involves hammers and nails. If you have younger children for whom this might be dangerous, you can attach a piece of fabric to the bottom of the cross and use a stapler.

Photocopy on to card and cut out enough of the red 'U-turn' arrows and enough of the white 'forgiveness' arrows for everyone to have one of each. Introduce the activity by explaining that when Jesus was killed, they nailed his hands and feet to the cross. It's a bit like nailing our sins to the cross, and that is what we are about to do.

The red arrow is a U-turn sign. It represents the times when we have made a U-turn away from God. Invite everyone either to write something they want to say sorry for on the back of a 'U-turn' arrow, or just nail or staple the card to the cross or to the fabric. Play some quiet music while everyone is doing this. After the participants have finished, give everyone a white 'forgiveness' arrow as they return to their seats. No words are needed—just the action.

Wipe the slate clean

You will need: a large cross, made from two pieces of cardboard or preferably thin wood, blackboard paint, a box of chalks and a damp cloth.

Before the session, paint the cross with the blackboard paint. Invite each person to draw on the cross a very simple picture to represent something that has broken: a heart, the name of someone they have fallen out with, a tree for the state of the planet and so on. Encourage everyone to do this as quietly as they can. This is an enjoyable activity, but it is also about saying sorry for the things we have done wrong. When each person has finished, hold the cross up and explain that because of this cross, which represents the cross of Jesus, all our sins have been wiped away. Receiving forgiveness means that the slate is wiped clean. As you are explaining this, take a damp cloth and wipe the cross clean.

Stones at the foot of the cross

The most effective aspect of this activity is that it has no words!

You will need: recent newspapers, paper, black felt-tipped pens, scissors, glue sticks, a display board or wall covered with strong paper, some large stones or small rocks and a large cross or crucifix.

Make a display of newspaper cuttings or print your own examples of things that are wrong: sins of the world, in the local community and in our own lives. Ensure that they include the sins we commit that do not hit the headlines, such as quarrelling, selfishness, cheating, dishonesty and so on. Arrange them so that they are linked—for example, personal rows linked with acts of war; cheating in an exam linked with a broken marriage; environmental disaster linked with wasting water.

The aim is to reflect on the sins that burden us and destroy relationships with God and each other. This is symbolized by taking a stone and placing it at the foot of the cross. There is always a danger in this kind of reflection that people may take responsibility for things for which they are not personally responsible, such as a war. The juxtaposition of the personal and communal sins is to remind us that although we cannot change the big things, we contribute to them by our own personal behaviour.

 ## Making Sunday special

Put the display in a focal point. Have a large cross standing near it or on the altar. Give each person a stone as they come into church: for practical reasons, most of these will be smaller than the ones used in the activity. After a time of reflection, invite people to lay the burden of sin at the foot of the cross.

An effective alternative is to put the headings on a PowerPoint presentation and play them during the time of reflection. This can be used as a penitential rite or in place of the intercessions.

Love God and love your neighbour

The aim of this activity is to show how God is the source of all love. We can receive his love and reflect it to other people by the way we live, or we can allow sin to come between us and him. The activity is very simple but needs a confident leader who has rehearsed in advance. It consists of demonstrating the effects of an eclipse of the sun and reflecting on the things that hide God's love from the world.

> **You will need:** a powerful torch, a disc of cardboard as big as or bigger than the torch's glass, and several small mirrors.

Start by drawing out what happens when there is an eclipse of the sun. Demonstrate it by directing the beam of light on to a wall or screen and then passing the disk slowly in front of the torch. (This is most effective in a darkened room.) If you are using the church, you may find that the building is dark enough if the lighting is turned off.

The activity leader explains that God's love is like the sun. We can receive it and reflect it to other people or, in the same way that the moon blocks out the sun during an eclipse, we can let sin come between God's love and us. The same effect is produced if we turn away from the light of his love. The leader could remind the group of the baptismal question and answer, 'Do you turn to Christ?' 'I turn to Christ.'

Invite a few of the people to take one of the mirrors each. Using the torch beam again, invite them to use the mirror to reflect the light around the church or room, even into dark corners and on to particular people. (Before you do this exercise, emphasize the danger of shining the light into other people's eyes.) Discuss how we can reflect God's love for us in the ways that we behave towards each other.

 ## Making Sunday special

This activity could form a penitential rite (especially in churches that read the two great commandments) or an interactive talk, especially on Sundays when there are readings from the Sermon on the Mount or when there is a baptism.

Reflection and prayer

Gather everyone together and, if possible, put the results of the various activities where they can be seen, or spend a few minutes walking around to look at them.

After a few minutes, ask the following questions:

✪ What have we experienced through doing the activities? *(Be prepared for some very personal replies at this point.)*
✪ How can we use what we have experienced during a Sunday Eucharist?
✪ Is there a place or opportunity to use what we have gained in another service or activity?

Light a candle and place it in the centre of the group. You might want to put some background music on and create a quiet atmosphere.

Further action and planning

See the 'Making Sunday special' suggestions for each of the activities. Discuss briefly which of the activities will be used in a future Sunday Eucharist, and arrange for a group of people to meet to implement the suggestions.

Note any ideas about a future penitential service—for example, in Holy Week—and be prepared to discuss them further.

Gospel

Stand up for Jesus!

Aim

To recognize that in the proclaiming of the Gospel, Jesus stands among us, present in his word, and to find creative ways of reading and reflecting on it.

Outline and suggested timing

The format of this workshop is slightly different in that the activities are directly based on two Bible readings. Each activity explores a different way of presenting or reflecting on a Gospel reading with a view to using the different styles in future services. There will probably be only enough time for each person to take part in a single activity, which will be either a dramatic performance of one of the Gospel readings or another creative activity. In order to allow time for the performances, the icebreaker is very short and the teaching on it is combined with the Bible readings. The suggested timing is as follows:

Icebreaker and welcome	10 mins	Activities	45 mins
Song	10 mins	Reflection	30 mins
Teaching and discussion	25 mins	Further action	10 mins
Refreshment break	15 mins	Notices	5 mins

Icebreaker

Either show one of the Gospel stories from Roly Bain's DVD, *The Gospel according to Roly*,[6] or have a number of different versions of the Gospels—Bibles, children's Bible stories, DVDs, films based on the Gospel such as *Jesus of Nazareth*[7]—for people to look at.

Song

Lord, thy word abideth (MP 446)
Out of darkness God has called us (CHE 639)
The light of Christ (CHE 703)
This little light of mine (CHE 736)
Seek ye first the kingdom of God (MP591)

Teaching and discussion

Read the following Gospel passages: Matthew 5:14–16 and John 9:1–17. Have copies prepared for each participant. You can download them free of charge from www.biblegateway.com.

These two Bible readings have a similar underlying theme: light and God being glorified. In the first reading, which is part of the Sermon on the Mount, Jesus is teaching about the way that his followers should live—that their good works are to the glory of God, like a light shining in darkness. The second reading is one of the healing miracles: Jesus explains that the man's blindness is not a result of sin, but that his healing gives an opportunity for God to be glorified.

Roly's presentation shows that there are many ways of telling the Gospel stories (as do the various books and DVDs that we have looked at). In spite of this rich variety and the vividness of the writing in almost any version, their impact is often destroyed by dull and lacklustre reading.

Draw out ways in which we already demonstrate the importance of the Gospel reading and that Jesus is present among us in his word. In the Anglican tradition, these include standing when the Gospel is proclaimed at the Eucharist.

In the following activities, we will take it a step further by finding different ways of proclaiming the Gospel and engaging with it.

Take a short break for refreshments at this point.

Activities

The suggested activities are divided into two groups: 'Proclaiming the Gospel', which comprises three dramatized versions of the two stories, and 'Engaging with the Gospel', which offers one reflective and two craft-based activities. We recommend that, unless the group is very small, at least one activity is chosen from each section. The dramas are designed to be rehearsed during this time in preparation for the 'Reflection and prayer' section.

Proclaiming the Gospel

A dramatized reading of John 9:1–12

John's account of the healing of the blind man lends itself well to dramatic reading as it has dialogue and a large number of contrasting characters. This version needs six or seven people to perform the dramatization.

For any dramatized reading, you will need either a copy of *The Dramatised Bible*[8] or copies of the text that have been clearly marked with the various parts. The story can be read with the exact text, or the directions such as 'He said...' can be omitted. In either case, the Evangelist (or storyteller) holds the reading together, but it is vital that speakers follow the text closely and are ready for their entries so that the reading keeps pace. Getting several people to speak together clearly takes a lot of rehearsal. Therefore, it may be preferable to have just one speaker to represent a crowd if rehearsal time is limited. It should take 20–30 minutes to rehearse the reading, but be prepared to allow more time if the readers are inexperienced.

Avoid having a group of people crowded around the lectern, sharing a microphone. It looks untidy and rarely produces good sound. It is better to stand the various characters in a row where they can be clearly seen—for example, on the chancel steps. If microphones are needed, it is best if each person has his or her own, or if a hand-held microphone is used, which is passed from person to person.

It is advisable to have the Evangelist standing in the pulpit, at the lectern or wherever the Gospel is usually proclaimed, and to have the usual introduction and response.

The following text is a dramatized version of the first part of the Gospel reading about the healing of the man born blind.

Characters
- Evangelist (storyteller)
- Jesus
- Blind man
- Disciples
- Two neighbours

Evangelist: As Jesus walked along, he saw a man who had been blind since birth.

Disciples: Teacher, why was this man born blind? Was it because he or his parents sinned?

Jesus: No, it wasn't! But, because of his blindness, you will see God perform a miracle for him. As long as it is day, we must do what the one who sent me wants me to do. When night comes, no one can work. While I am in the world, I am the light for the world.

Reproduced with permission from *Creative Communion* published by BRF 2008 (978 1 84101 533 0) www.barnabasinchurches.org.uk

Evangelist:	Then Jesus spat on the ground. He made some mud and smeared it on the man's eyes.
Jesus:	Go and wash off the mud in Siloam Pool.
Evangelist:	The man went and washed in Siloam, which means, 'One who is sent'. When he had washed off the mud, he could see. The man's neighbours and the people who had seen him begging wondered if he really could be the same man.
Neighbour 1:	He's the same beggar.
Neighbour 2:	No, he only looks like him!
Blind man:	I am that man.
Neighbours:	Then how can you see?
Blind man:	Someone named Jesus made some mud and smeared it on my eyes. He told me to go and wash it off in Siloam Pool. When I did, I could see.
Neighbours:	Where is he now?
Blind man:	I don't know.

A mime to illustrate a reading of John 9:1–12

This mime is to be acted out during the reading about Jesus healing the man who was born blind. The movements are simple and can be rehearsed in about 30–40 minutes. If the whole church area can be used, it adds to the effect of the blind man having to travel to the Siloam Pool and being taken to see the Pharisees. A reader and five other people are needed for the mime.

If the reader cannot see the action, it is helpful to have a prompter hidden behind a pillar to signal when he or she should continue the narrative. As with the dramatized reading, you can emphasize that this is a proclamation of the Gospel by having it read from the usual place with the usual introduction and responses.

Characters
- Reader (Evangelist)
- Jesus
- Blind man
- Disciples
- Two neighbours

The **Reader** says, 'Hear a reading from the Gospel according to John' and begins to read the passage. The movements during the narration are as follows.

Verse 1: *The blind man is seated with eyes closed and hand outstretched for alms. Enter Jesus and his disciples. One of the disciples points to the blind man. Jesus turns to face his disciples to teach.*

Verse 6: *Jesus squats on the ground, spits and makes mud. The disciples stand back. Jesus walks over to the blind man, who lifts his head. Jesus smears mud over the blind man's eyes. Jesus takes him by the hand and helps him to stand up.*

Verse 7: *Jesus points to the pool. One of the disciples leads the blind man towards it. Together they wash off the mud. The blind man blinks and slowly looks around. Then he walks unaided back to centre stage. Exit Jesus and disciples.*

Verse 8: *Enter the neighbours, who go up to the man and ask questions.*

Verse 9: *The man replies by nodding his head and pointing to himself.*

Verse 11: *The man mimes Jesus putting mud on his eyes, and then makes a washing motion. He smiles and stretches out his hands.*

Verse 12: *The neighbours lean forward and look around. The blind man shakes his head and shrugs his shoulders. Exit the blind man and the neighbours.*

The **Reader** finishes with the words, 'This is the Gospel of the Lord.'

A dramatized reading of Matthew 5:14–16

This dramatization is based on the parable of the lamp.

Characters
- ☼ Evangelist (a clear reader)
- ☼ Lost person (the only real actor)
- ☼ Lamplighter (a non-speaking part, but the character needs to move slowly with a sense of occasion as his or her actions tell the first part of the story)
- ☼ Representatives of various ministries (see script for examples)

Props
- ☼ Large candle
- ☼ A cover for the candle (this can be a tall cylinder of black card, but there must be an opening at the top to prevent the card from igniting or the candle going out)
- ☼ A small table or candle stand
- ☼ Small candles and holders (one for each ministry being represented)
- ☼ A taper

The large candle (unlit) is placed off-centre, but must be visible to the whole congregation. Once it has been lit as part of the dramatized reading, it should stay lit for the rest of the service if possible. The cover is on the floor beside the stand. The room (or church) should be unlit. The Evangelist stands at the lectern with the Bible open.

Lost person: (*Starting from the back of the room or church, gropes his or her way to the front*) Oh, it's so dark. I'm not sure where I am. (*Calls out*) Where am I? Is anyone there? Can I have some light?

Enter the lamplighter carrying a lighted taper, with which he or she lights the candle. He or she then places the candle on the table or candle stand, steps back one pace and looks at it approvingly.

Lost person: Oh, that is better. I'm in some sort of building.

The lamplighter steps forward, lifts the candle cover from the floor, places it over the light, and exits.

Lost person: That isn't much use. I can't see where I am again.

Evangelist: Jesus said, 'You are like light for the whole world. A city built on top of a hill cannot be hidden, and no one would light a lamp and put it under a clay pot. A lamp is placed on a lampstand, where it can give light to everyone in the house.

Enter the lamplighter. He or she removes the cover from the light.

Lost person: Oh, now I can see where I am! I'm in…
(names the building).

A child comes forward with a small unlit candle. The lamplighter lights it from the large candle, using the taper.

Child: I belong to… *(names the church's children's group)*

Congregation: And God be glorified.*

Continue this pattern with a representative of each ministry—for example, a member of the prayer ministry team; missionary team, pastoral team, youth team, children's team, outreach team and so on.

Evangelist: In the same way, your light must shine before people, so that they will see the good things you do and glorify* your Father in heaven.

At the end of the service, before the blessing, ask the representatives of the various ministries to come forward for their candles to be lit again. At the dismissal, the deacon or priest says, 'Let us go in peace to let our lights shine in the world to the glory of God.' The people with candles then process out of the church to show that they are going out as lights into the world to the glory of God.

*NB: Some translations of the text say 'glorify' your Father, and others say 'praise'. It is important that the same word is used in the response to the ministry representatives as in the Evangelist's reading. The emphasis must be that our good works are to proclaim the glory of God, not to demonstrate how busy and successful the church is.

Reproduced with permission from *Creative Communion* published by BRF 2008 (978 1 84101 533 0) www.barnabasinchurches.org.uk

Engaging with the Gospel

Making a newspaper

> **You will need:** a personal computer or large sheets of paper and pens.

Imagine that you are a news reporter and you have been asked to write a front page news story about the event in the Gospel story. Your task is:

- To design the front page of the newspaper.
- To work out a strapline for the story, which will catch the reader's eye.
- To write a report of about 200 words about what you saw. You can even imagine interviewing people who were witnesses to the event. Try to think about their feelings and emotions and 'paint a picture' in your writing. Think about the difference the event made to the people.

Art work

For this activity, your task is to create a piece of artwork that will illustrate either one of the stories or the theme of darkness and light. A group could work on an altar frontal together or could make a number of simple banners.

The simplest work is done on light card with paint and felt-tipped pens. More experienced people could build up collages on cloth using items such as pieces of fabric, felt, trimmings and sequins fastened with adhesive. Whatever you decide to do, you will need a large space in which to work, preferably with tables, although it is possible to use the floor. You will also need newspaper to protect surfaces, and facilities for washing brushes and hands.

The following instructions are for the simplest versions:

✪ **A frontal:** You will need sheets of lightweight card stuck together to fit the front of the altar, poster paints, palettes and large brushes.

✪ **Banners:** The simplest banners are made with A3 card or heavy paper and are ideal for children or for adults who do not feel confident using craft materials. Larger banners need stronger construction, but the principle is the same. For each banner, you will need a sheet of A3 card or paper, one long and one or two short garden canes, masking tape, paints, brushes and felt-tipped pens.

The design can be created at the time, but it is better to have it drawn on the frontal or large banner before the activity. Small banners can be made with outline drawings on sheets of A3 paper or card. When finished, the banners are stuck to the canes with masking tape.

Lectio divina

Lectio divina is a way of reading the Bible using silence and the imagination and through listening and repeating, allowing God to speak to us through our silence and meditation.

Ask everyone to sit quietly in a circle, and explain that they are going to listen to a Bible reading three times.

After the first time, ask everyone to do nothing except think what his or her favourite words were in the reading. They may only choose one word or a very short phrase.

Ask everyone to listen to the reading again. This time, invite each person in turn to say his or her favourite word or phrase. You could make it a bit like 'pass the parcel' by passing a Bible around. When each person is given the Bible, they just speak out their word.

Listen to the reading for the third time, and then pass the Bible to one another again, this time inviting people to talk about what they were imagining about the word and why that particular word or phrase was so special to them.

Explain that it doesn't matter if people choose the same word; what it means to each individual is the important thing.

You could adapt the session by inviting each person to write his or her responses in the style of a graffiti wall.

Reflection and prayer

Allow a full half hour for the reflection so that there is time to perform one of the dramas. Ask the following questions:

✪ What have we learnt about the importance of proclaiming the Gospel effectively?
✪ What has stuck us about the particular readings and their messages?
✪ Do we want to use these particular readings in a service or use the experience to make other Gospel readings more effective?

Light a candle and place it with an open Bible in the centre of the group.

Almighty God, We thank you for the gift of your holy word. May it be a lamp to our feet, a light wherever we walk, and may it give strength to our lives. Take us and use us to love and serve you in the power of your Holy Spirit and in the name of your Son, Jesus Christ our Lord.

Further action and planning

Discuss briefly which of the activities will be used in a future Sunday Eucharist or whether the techniques learned will be used on other Gospel readings. Arrange for a group of people to meet to implement the suggestions.

Offering

It's all yours!

Aim

To introduce creative ways of praying for the world and also of offering ourselves to God.

Outline and suggested timing

See page 50 for information, but as there is a short piece of teaching attached to the refreshment time, you will need to allow a few minutes longer at that point.

Icebreaker

Play one of the following games.

On offer!

Sit in a circle and throw a soft ball to each other. As each person throws it, they use the words, 'I offer...' Each person then contributes something that he or she values or feels they are good at. For example, 'I offer... my swimming' '... my maths' '... my work' '... my helping others' '... my smile' and so on.

Any soft ball will do, but use a large one if possible so that small children and elderly people can easily join in. CMS (Church Mission Society) produces a globe-shaped stress ball in different sizes. It has

'CMS' and 'God's love is meant to be shared' written around it. It can be purchased from CMS at www.cms-shop.co.uk.

> **Teaching point**
> Everyone is good at something and brings something to the table. We all have something to offer. This session looks at how we offer our prayers and how we offer ourselves.

Reaching out!

Sit in a circle and throw a globe-shaped stress ball or an inflatable globe to each other. If you wish to use a large inflatable globe or earth ball, your diocesan or local education department may have one that can be borrowed.

Alternatively, a large range of earth balls and similar resources can be found on www.mapshop.com/Geography_for_Kids.cfm.

As you throw the globe around the group, ask each person to name a place or country in the world that is special. Encourage people to choose a place that no one else has mentioned.

> **Teaching point**
> When everyone has had a go, point out that when we are thinking about prayers, we are not just thinking about ourselves but about how much God loves the world. Our prayers are not just about what we want but also about what other people in the world need.

Song

All that I am (CHE 23)
Blessed are you, Lord God of all creation (CHE 90)

I will bring to you the best gift I can offer (Come and Praise, BBC)
I will offer up my life (TS 265)

Teaching and discussion

Read John 6:1–13, the story of the feeding of the five thousand. This teaching activity comprises a quiet, reflective Bible study, helping everyone to imagine that he or she is there, to think about what it is like to offer what each of us has, and to recognize what Jesus can do with it. Read the story quietly and at a slow pace. The instructions in brackets are to be read in the same manner.

Invite people to get themselves into a comfortable position, close their eyes if they wish to do so, and imagine the scene.

There is a hillside and it is crowded with people as far as the eye can see—as many as at a football match or big event you might have been to or seen on TV.

Imagine being part of the crowd. You are really hungry. Your tummy is rumbling. (*Rub your tummy now…*)

No one has any food and Jesus and his disciples are worried that there is not enough to feed the crowd. No one around you has brought any food… except you! In your packed lunch box are five bread rolls and two fresh fish. You hold up your packed lunch. (*Hold it up now…*) You say to one of the disciples, Andrew, 'Here, have my lunch!' (*Say those words now…*) He doesn't hear you. So you say it louder: 'Here, have my lunch!' (*Say it again…*) He still doesn't hear you! So you shout it out until he responds. (*Shout it out!*)

Andrew takes what you have and offers it to Jesus. You can just see that Jesus is saying a prayer. Then he offers the bread and fish that you have brought and hands it round.

Now imagine you can see everyone eating lots and lots. (*You, too, take some food and eat it now…*)

Just then you realize… that yours was the only food to be offered. 'Wow!' you whisper to yourself. (*Whisper 'wow' now… then whisper 'wow' again—even quieter this time*) It was from your little offering that everyone had enough to eat.

After a pause, invite everyone to open their eyes. Explain that all those people were fed because one boy offered his lunch to Jesus. Remember the gift we said we were offering in the opening game? Jesus gave us those gifts to use for others. How might we each use our gifts to share with others?

Have a short discussion about the gifts that each of us has, the things we are good at, and how those things can be shared for the benefit of others. You might want to refer back to the globe by pointing out areas of the world in particular need, and say that when we offer our gifts it is not just for those around us but also for the whole world.

Refreshment break

Instead of having everyone just coming for a drink, or putting the drinks out, ask everyone to sit in a circle. Offer the drinks and biscuits and pass them round. Does it feel good or bad being offered something? Just as we have enjoyed receiving a drink and a biscuit, Jesus enjoys receiving our gifts and wants to give us more in return.

Activities

Before starting the activities, ask, 'What is the difference between praying and interceding? Why do we have intercessions and not just prayers?'

The activities come under two headings: intercessions and offertory.

If possible, ensure that at least one activity from each section is used and that each person has a chance to take part in both an intercession activity and one about the offertory.

Intercession activities

Bubble prayers

You will need: some small pots of bubble-blowing liquid.

Invite everyone to imagine that the person or situation they want to pray for is captured in one of the bubbles. As the bubbles are blown, let everyone watch as the bubbles are taken up into God's hands. You can work through different themes of prayer, such as the Church, the world, people you know and so on.

Balloon prayers

You will need: pens, inflated balloons, luggage labels and a large net.

Invite everyone to write an intercession on a luggage label and attach it to a balloon. Gather all the balloons together in a large net. Take the net of balloons into the open air and then, after a short prayer, such as, 'Loving Father God, accept these prayers for the sake of Jesus Christ our Lord. Amen', toss the balloons into the air. If you are able to fill the balloons with helium gas, it will work even better.

Teaspoon prayers

You will need: plastic teaspoons, permanent markers.

The abbreviation for teaspoon is 'tsp', which could stand for 'thank you', 'sorry' and 'please'. Invite people to say thank you for something as they write a 'T' on the spoon. Then invite people to say (either out loud or quietly) something they want to say sorry for as they write an 'S' on the spoon. Finally, invite people to put their requests to God (not for themselves, but for someone they know, their families or a situation they are worried about in the world) as they write a 'P' on the spoon.

To gather these prayers together, you could bring them up in a basket or bag and place them on the altar or Communion table as part of the offertory. You say a similar prayer to the one in 'Balloon prayers', beginning with the words, 'Loving Father God...'.

Candle prayers

Invite people to gather round a lit candle. If you can make the room darker and more atmospheric, so much the better. Look at the flame. It represents light and warmth. It is a light shining in the darkness. Then simply ask people who and what they would like to pray for. It might be for someone who is sad or feels that life is dark and gloomy, or for an unfair situation that needs resolving. Allow the participants to voice their prayers or simply to pray in the silence of their hearts.

At the end, gather the prayers with a conclusion such as, 'Lord God, you are the light for the world. We offer our prayers to you and pray that you would shine your light on all the people and situations we have thought about or spoken about. Amen.'

Four points of the compass

This form of prayer is designed to take place in the open air or in a building with large windows. It encourages people to look and even move as they are praying, rather than burying their heads in their hands. The person leading the prayers invites people to:

- ✪ Look up. See the world, the beauty of creation… (thanksgiving)
- ✪ Look at the ground. It is dirty and rough. It reminds us of the things that are bad in the world and in our lives… (penitence)
- ✪ Point the right arm sideways with the hand outstretched… (intercession: prayer for others)
- ✪ Hold the left arm sideways and bend the hand and wrist towards themselves… (supplication: prayer for ourselves)

Offertory activities

Mirrors

You will need: A large framed mirror, pens, some Post-it notes and a large red paper heart.

Explain that in the offertory we are offering ourselves. In quite a lot of churches, this is symbolized by people bringing forward the bread and wine and money offerings, but this is not what the offertory is actually about. It is all about the offering of ourselves to God. God wants us because he believes that we are the most precious things that he has created. That is why we are going to offer ourselves, and one way to do this is to remind ourselves of how God sees us.

Display the large framed mirror. Ask people to imagine that God is looking at them. Invite them to think what is the loveliest thing anyone could say about them. Encourage them to voice their thoughts if they would like to, and write the suggestions on the mirror, or on Post-it notes to be stuck on the mirror. You might want to stick the notes all around the outside of the mirror, so that what God is saying about each person surrounds the image of whoever is looking at themselves.

Finally, stick a huge red heart on the mirror as a reminder that no matter what we or others might think of us, God views us with total love and wants us to offer ourselves as we are, to be used for God.

The story of bread and wine

This dramatic presentation aims to help the congregation to see the offertory as a moment to offer their whole selves to God.

> **You will need:** costumes for various characters (see below), a large loaf of bread and a bottle of wine laid on or in front of the altar or Communion table, and a simple script (see below) to introduce the characters. This can be developed further as time and talent allow.

The first story is about making bread, from the sowing of seed to the delivery of bread to the shop.

Reader 1: The farmer sows the seed and cuts the wheat...
The lorry driver takes it to a mill...
The miller grinds it into flour...
The baker bakes the flour into bread...
The van driver delivers it to the shop...

So, we see that the bread we offer represents our work as well as being a basic food.

The second story shows us some of the various celebrations at which wine is drunk.

Reader 2: Wine is drunk to celebrate a wedding... *(bridal clothes)*
a sporting event... *(sports kit)*
an 18th birthday... *(young people's clothes)*
a business lunch... *(dark suits)*

Wine is used in celebrations as well as being a drink made of fermented grapes.

Reproduced with permission from *Creative Communion* published by BRF 2008 (978 1 84101 533 0) **www.barnabasinchurches.org.uk**

As the script is read, each character moves to stand around the altar or Communion table, beginning on the President's right for the bread and on his or her left for the wine. The bread and wine may then be brought forward from the congregation, accompanied by quiet music or by singing the hymn, 'Blest are you Lord God of all creation' (see the list of songs above). The characters could remain around the altar for the Eucharistic Prayer.

Reflection and prayer

❂ What have we learnt about the offering of our intercessions?
❂ Was there any particular prayer activity that we might want to use at some time?
❂ Which of the offertory presentations might we want to use in a service? Do they inspire any further ideas?

Light a candle and place it with the globe in the centre of the group. If you have not used a globe ball in the icebreaker, place an atlas of the world there instead. Use either the candle prayer or the four points of the compass prayer. Conclude with the following prayer from 1 Chronicles 29:11 (NRSV):

Yours, O Lord, are the greatness,
the power, the glory, the victory, and the majesty;
for all that is in the heavens and on the earth is yours;
yours is the kingdom, O Lord,
and you are exalted as head above all.

Further action and planning

Arrange to feed back what has been learnt to the person or group in charge of the intercessions for the Sunday services. Discuss when or where some of the activities can be used. Decide whether the offertory activities can be used for a Sunday Eucharist or, for example, as part of a harvest thanksgiving service.

Eucharistic Prayer

Food for the journey: Eating in

Aim

To show the importance and centrality of sharing Holy Communion regularly together without taking it for granted.

Outline and suggested timing

See page 50 for information. **NB**: The Reflection section will take longer than usual, so watch the timing carefully. The further planning will be shorter, so it should be possible to keep to the basic timescale.

Icebreaker

Invite people to imagine that they have as much money as they want to spend on a meal, and they can have two types of food. What would they dream up? Save some money for decorations: what would they do to decorate the food and the table?

Ask everyone to get into pairs or small groups or to work as families to plan their dream meals. Then ask each group or family in turn to present their meal and the decoration.

Song

Eat this bread (Taizé) (CHE 151)
Gather us in (CHE 253)
Holy, holy (MP 238)
I am the bread of life (CHE 272)

Teaching and discussion

Read 1 Corinthians 11:23–29. These are the words that Jesus used at the last supper. Paul is reminding his readers that this is a very important meal and is not to be taken lightly. Most of the special eucharistic prayers we use in church are based on this passage. We have different prayers for different occasions, but some of the words are the same as in the Bible. We are going to look at one of the prayers to help us: Eucharistic Prayer H from *Common Worship* (see page 159).

This Eucharistic Prayer will be used as the basis for teaching, which will lead into some of the activities. The Eucharistic Prayer is often quite long, but there are lots of interesting and important things about it. It is a big prayer, which the President says on our behalf, so we need to take part in it. Eucharist means 'thanksgiving', so it is a big 'thank you' prayer. What are we saying 'thank you' to God for?

Part One of the prayer is a big 'thank you' for the great works of God in creation. Ask everyone to suggest some of the amazing things that God has made. Write down on a large sheet of paper the collective suggestions. If 'human beings' is not among them, mention it and talk about how we have been made in God's image. The prayer talks about how welcome we are at the table, no matter what we have done wrong.

Next, ask everyone what is the biggest gift that God has given to us. The prayer talks about the gift of Jesus dying (being broken) and then coming back to life.

Part Two of the prayer recalls the last meal that Jesus had with his friends, and the words he used. (These are the words in the Bible reading.) Ask everyone to recall the party food they had in the icebreaker session. The two special parts of this Communion meal are bread and wine. Talk about different things to do with bread. What can we make from it? (Sandwiches, bread sauce, breadcrumbs, pizza, savoury crumble, toast and so on.) You could also talk about different types of bread, such as pitta, naan or rye. Ask everyone when was the last time they ate bread. Most people have probably eaten bread that day and eat it every day. It is a staple diet for many people. Bread represents Jesus' body: it is the visual aid that Jesus uses so that whenever we eat bread we think of him.

Talk about what happens to the bread in the Eucharist:

✪ It is blessed. When we have something precious and important, we mark its importance by treating it in a special way. By blessing the bread, we are praying that God would use it for his purposes: it is a special sign, pointing us to God.
✪ It is broken as a reminder that Jesus' life was broken for us when he was put to death.
✪ It is shared: Jesus reminds us that we are not members of a private club; he wants to share himself with the whole world.

We do the same with the wine as a symbol of Jesus' blood.

Part Three of the prayer is the invocation of the Holy Spirit. In every Eucharistic Prayer, there is a point at which we call on the Holy Spirit to bless and make special the bread and wine. Ask everyone to think about someone they have met who they think is amazing. It could be a friend, a football hero, a dancer, or someone who has suffered an illness and is being very brave.

Sometimes, when we meet someone, they change us: we want to be like them because of the encounter. You might want to tell a personal story here about someone you have met who has had an impact on you. When you have told your story, invite the group to wonder what might happen if we invited Jesus to meet us. How might that meeting change us? Ask people how they might be changed. Would they be more like Jesus? Would it be a good or bad experience?

In the Eucharistic Prayer—this big 'thank you' prayer—there is a special moment when we call on the Holy Spirit to change the bread and wine to be to us Jesus' body and blood. The bread and wine have an added value: they are extra special because it is as if they have been soaked in Jesus' love and blessing. We become like Jesus as we eat things that are blessed by Jesus.

The final part of the prayer, Part Four, is a big song of thanks. Because this is a big 'thank you' prayer, which is used by Christians all over the world, we join with them in a special song. When we sing, everyone in heaven joins in a 'thank you' song about God. Go round the group, asking them to shout out something they want to say 'thank you' for and then use this pattern and the following refrain for as long as you like. Make sure that the Hosannas are shouted with real gusto.

Thank you, God of power and might, for this food and…
Hosanna in the highest!

Take a short break for refreshments at this point.

Activities

The big frieze

This activity can be done in various ways and follows on from the teaching. The aim is to make a pictorial frieze, which can be displayed around the church or made into a scroll.

You will need: a roll of lining wallpaper (unpasted), two large tubes (such as poster tubes), paints, paintbrushes and sticky tape.

You can make the frieze in six sections and express in art and drawing what is going on in the Eucharistic Prayer. Then, at the next service of Holy Communion, someone can scroll down each section as the prayer progresses so that the images correspond to the words and actions.

When you have finished designing your frieze, decorate each section. You might want to get different groups to work on the sections. The six sections are as follows:

✪ Thanks for the mighty works of God in creation.
✪ Thanks for making human beings.
✪ Thanks for the gift of Jesus' life and death on the cross.
✪ The words of the Last Supper.
✪ The invocation of the Holy Spirit to bless the bread and wine.
✪ The song of praise.

Work on the sections and, when they are dry, join them together with strong tape. Finally, attach one end of the finished frieze to one of the tubes. Roll the frieze up around this tube and attach the other end to the second tube.

Remember, re-member!

You will need: a large piece of card (A2 sized if possible), a piece of paper of the same size, felt-tipped pens and PVA glue.

Before the session begins, draw a simple outline of a Communion setting on the piece of paper—people gathered around the table, with bread and wine and so on.

In the Eucharistic Prayer, we say, 'Do this in remembrance that Christ died for you' and 'Do this in remembrance that Christ's blood was shed for you.' Can you think of another time when we use the word 'remembrance'? Remembrance Sunday is about remembering all those who have died for us to keep us in peace. To help us remember, we wear poppies and say special prayers. Sometimes we think that, in the same way, Holy Communion is about reminding ourselves of all that God has done for us. But it is more than recall! The opposite of the word 'remember' is not 'forget', but 'dismember' —that is, to pull apart.

Make a jigsaw template of a Communion setting. Invite everyone to help colour in the picture. When it is finished, back it on to card and cut it into large irregular pieces. The jigsaw could be used in an offertory procession. As we bring up the different gifts, we bring up the pieces of jigsaw and become the body of Christ as we form the shape of the picture on the table.

Baking bread

You will need: enough bread-making mix (available from any supermarket, or you can make your own) for everyone to make two small rolls, some water, large mixing bowls and spoons, baking sheets and some small plastic bags. You will also need the availability of an oven.

Preheat the oven at the beginning of the activity. Following the instructions on the packet, or the recipe, invite everyone to make two bread rolls—one to take home and the other to give to a friend as a reminder that Jesus shared himself not just with us but with everyone. Everyone is welcome at his table. Remember to save some of the bread if it is to be used in the Reflection section.

Loose juice

You will need: soft red fruits such as strawberries, raspberries, redcurrants or red grapes; a juicer, blender or smoothie maker; a large jug and some plastic cups.

In this activity, we are going to make some fruit juice to represent the wine of Holy Communion. Ask some of the participants to make up a red-coloured fruit cocktail. Mix up the fruit in the juicer or blender and then add some water so that there is enough juice to go round for the Reflection section.

Eucharistic Prayer stopwatch

> **You will need**: stiff paper cut into large circles, some cardboard, scissors, a split-pin fastener, pencils and felt-tipped pens.

Cut out a large circle of paper. Fold it in half, then in half again, and then in half again. Unfold it and you will have eight segments. In one of them write, 'The big thank you prayer'. Then, on each of the other segments, draw one of the following items:

✪ Something from creation
✪ A person
✪ Jesus on the cross
✪ Bread and wine
✪ A symbol of the Holy Spirit
✪ Anything to express praise
✪ The word 'Amen'

Cut out a simple cardboard arrow and fix it in the centre of the paper circle with a split-pin fastener.

Prayer stopwatches are useful for younger children to use during the Eucharistic Prayer, as they can move the arrow round as they hear words that match the picture, segment by segment.

Reflection and prayer

This session should be concluded with an act of Holy Communion, using some of the bread, juice and other items that have been made in the activities.

In a sense, this whole session is an extended service of Holy Communion. The liturgy of the word was included in the Teaching and Discussion session, so it is appropriate now to gather around a decorated table and begin with the Eucharistic Prayer. (See Appendix One for the suggested version.) This is an interactive Eucharistic Prayer, so everyone will need copies of the text, or you can put the words on a PowerPoint or overhead projector. Try to avoid using service sheets, as everyone needs to engage visually without the encumbrance of pieces of paper.

At the end of the prayer, sing the song you sang at the beginning of the session, say the Lord's Prayer together and then invite everyone to share some bread and juice.

End with a post-Communion prayer, such as the one below.

Loving and generous God, thank you so much for letting us share in this wonderful feast, which you have given to us. Thank you for the food and for what it means to us. Thank you that your love takes away our hunger. Help us to share ourselves with others as you have shared yourself with us. Amen

Further action and planning

Arrange to display some of the activities in the church. Ask the children's leaders (if not present) whether they would like the Eucharistic Prayer stopwatch for the children to use, or the opportunity to make their own.

As this session has been more reflective and has explored the core of the Eucharist, there will probably not be any requests for changes or additions to the service in the near future. There may well be, however, requests to discuss issues surrounding Holy Communion, including whether children should receive it (if they do not already do so), Christian initiation and the ecumenical dimension. These topics should be welcomed, but time and space will be needed for teaching and full discussion.

6

Dismissal

Food for the journey: Take away

Icebreaker

You will need a rucksack as a visual aid for this memory game. The idea is to remember what the last person said and add an extra thing to put in the rucksack. To vary the game, you could challenge people to add a new word beginning with the next letter of the alphabet. You can pass the rucksack around as well, if you like.

Start by saying, 'I'm going on a hike in the wild woods, and in my rucksack I am going to take…'

At the end, make the point that you now have loads of stuff in the rucksack. We always take too much with us when we go on holiday—something for every eventuality. We travel heavy. In Holy

Communion, when we leave, we go with God's word and bread and wine as God's food for our journey. This 'food' is not heavy, but it is the most precious thing we can take with us. The dismissal of the service is about carrying this provision out of church—and we are the rucksacks in which God has chosen to carry himself.

Song

We are marching (MP 718)
You shall go out with joy (MP 796)
Go forth and tell (MP 178)
We have a gospel to proclaim (CHE 778)

Teaching and discussion

Read Luke 24:13–35. This is a long reading, so we suggest that it is dramatized in a way that engages with the change in the disciples through their encounter with Jesus. If you are meeting in a large hall or room, put two large signs on opposite walls—one saying 'Jerusalem' and the other 'Emmaus'. If the weather is fine, it works really well to do the drama outdoors in a playing field, with signs at either end, hung on a goalpost or a tree.

The narration below is taken from THE MESSAGE.

That same day two of them were walking to the village Emmaus, about seven miles out of Jerusalem. They were deep in conversation, going over all these things that had happened. In the middle of their talk and questions, Jesus came up and walked along with them. But they were not able to recognize who he was. He asked, 'What's this you're discussing so intently as you walk along?' They just stood there, long-faced, like they had lost their best friend. Then one of them, his name was Cleopas, said, 'Are you the only one in Jerusalem who hasn't heard what's happened during the last few days?' He said, 'What has happened?'

Start with everyone standing just outside Jerusalem. Which way are they facing? Emmaus is some distance from Jerusalem, so invite everyone to turn their backs on Jerusalem and face Emmaus. Ask how they might be feeling if Jesus had just died and he was a very close friend. Would they be happy or sad? How would they be walking? Invite people to do a sad walk for a few steps.

They said, 'The things that happened to Jesus the Nazarene. He was a man of God, a prophet, dynamic in work and word, blessed by both God and all the people. Then our high priests and leaders betrayed him, got him sentenced to death, and crucified him. And we had our hopes up that he was the One, the One about to deliver Israel. And it is now the third day since it happened. But now some of our women have completely confused us. Early this morning they were at the tomb and couldn't find his body. They came back with the story that they had seen a vision of angels who said he was alive. Some of our friends went off to the tomb to check and found it empty just as the women said, but they didn't see Jesus.'

Then he said to them, 'So thick-headed! So slow-hearted! Why can't you simply believe all that the prophets said? Don't you see that these things had to happen, that the Messiah had to suffer and only then enter into his glory?' Then he started at the beginning, with the Books of Moses, and went on through all the Prophets, pointing out everything in the Scriptures that referred to him.

'Thick-headed?' That's a bit cheeky! But sometimes we are a bit slow. Invite everyone to scratch his or her head and look confused. Take a few more steps closer to Emmaus. Perhaps have a little competition to find the person looking the most thick-headed!

They came to the edge of the village where they were headed. He acted as if he was going on but they pressed him: 'Stay and have supper with us. It's nearly evening; the day is done.' So he went in with them. And here is what happened: He sat down at the table with them. Taking the bread, he blessed and broke and gave it to them. At that moment, open-eyed, wide-eyed, they recognized him. And then he disappeared.

Invite everyone to walk to where the Emmaus sign is. Mime the phrase 'Stay with us' with a beckoning arm or an invitation. Then bring in a bottle of wine or juice and a loaf of bread and place them in the middle of the group. Imagine the look on the disciples' faces as they recognized that all this time it had been Jesus with them. Their best friend had come back to life! Ask people how they would react. Would they be open-eyed? Wide-eyed? Staring? Cheering? Jumping for joy? Invite people to do whatever they want to do.

Back and forth they talked. 'Didn't we feel on fire as he conversed with us on the road, as he opened up the Scriptures for us?'

They didn't waste a minute. They were up and on their way back to Jerusalem. They found the Eleven and their friends gathered together, talking away: 'It's really happened! The Master has been raised up—Simon saw him!'

Then the two went over everything that happened on the road and how they recognized him when he broke the bread.

Invite everyone to run back to Jerusalem and shout, 'We have seen Jesus! We have seen Jesus! Jesus is alive!'

Get everyone to sit down where they are, under the Jerusalem sign. Compare how they are feeling now (as disciples) to how they were feeling at the start of the journey. At the beginning, they were sad and talking about things among themselves. Now, at the end of the journey, they are not just talking to themselves, but sharing everything that has happened with their friends. Their hearts are on fire and they want to share and tell everyone. This is the result of sharing bread and wine in the presence of Jesus.

That is what we are called to do as Christians. Once we have received, we are called to share and give the love we have received to others.

Refreshments

As you are having a drink break, share some good news that has happened to you this week with somebody else.

Activities

Choose one of the following activities.

Egg box elements

You will need: an empty egg box for each person,: paper, card, a small box, silver paper, glue sticks and a Communion wafer or small piece of bread.

There are six things to make which bring together the elements of Holy Communion:

❂ Make a small paper chain of just three pieces of paper (each approximately 2cm x 10cm) joined together.

❂ Using a small piece of card (the size of a 10p piece), draw a sad face on one side and a smiley face on the other to signify saying sorry and forgiveness.

❂ Make a small book to symbolize the scriptures out of pieces of paper (about 3cm x 2cm) cut out, folded in half and stapled together.

❂ Either cut out a small set of two hands as an offertory or decorate a small box and wrap it up as a symbol of the gift we offer to God.

❂ Make a small chalice out of silver paper (a sweet wrapper is just the right size for this) and use a Communion wafer or small piece of bread.

❂ On a small piece of card, draw around a 1p coin three times, one circle under another, to look like traffic lights. To symbolize the dismissal, colour in the green light and write the word 'go' in the other two circles (put the 'g' where the red light would be, and the 'o' where the amber light would be).

Encourage people to decorate their egg boxes with the words 'My creative Communion box' and paint or design both the outside and the inside.

NB: Anyone who finds intricate craft work difficult could make a larger version using a shoebox. Divide the box with the dividers found in cases of wine. You can sometimes find empty cases with other boxes by the supermarket checkout.

Take away bags

You will need: small paper bags with handles, either homemade or bought from a local wholesaler or a takeaway restaurant.

Ask people what they would want to put in their bags. Suggest things to help us grow in the faith, such as a small notebook, a bag of seeds, or a cut-out of a hand. (You could invite everyone to draw around his or her hand, cut out the shape and write, 'I want to offer help to someone this week by...') Other items might include a small packet of Love Hearts (using the sweets as an illustration, work out how we might carry out some of the more appropriate instructions), sweets to share or Bible promises written out on small pieces of paper (for example, 'I will be with you always').

Oikos cards

The word *oikos* is Greek for 'extended household' or 'network' of relationships. In the New Testament, much of the evangelism is *oikos*-based.

Sharing all that God has given to us is about praying for specific people. Hand out cards made up as specified below, and invite people to think of three others they could pray for, whom they know, like well and see often.

My contacts who are loved by God
and for whom I have a special concern:

_____

_____

_____

Ask people to be alert for opportunities to be a witness by praying for these people, thinking about how they can serve them and how they can talk to them about the Christian faith.

Reflection and prayer

The departure gate

Have a table set with a cross, a Bible and some bread and wine. You will also need some tealight candles, a box of matches and a taper, and a train or plane ticket for each person with the words, 'One return ticket to feed the world' printed on it.

For this big farewell, you will also need to set up rows of seats as if they were a compartment in a train or plane. Place the words 'Arrival Gate' or 'Way Out' over a door as if it were an airport or train station.

Invite everyone to sit down as if they were in a train carriage or plane. Set the scene by asking everyone to imagine they are on a train or plane. They could mime landing or coming into a station with noises and gestures. Explain that on planes and trains you get departure and arrival announcements, which go something like this:

Thank you for travelling with Pilgrimage Airways (insert your own imaginary train or air company). We hope that you have had a pleasant flight (or trip). Please don't forget to take all your belongings with you; we wish you a safe onward journey.

The dismissal or conclusion of the service is a bit like one of those announcements, but the most important thing is that we take all that we have been given with us for our onward journey—at home, at school or at work, and with our friends and family.

Ask the group to think about what we take away from a service of Holy Communion. What have we made today and been reminded of? How can we carry these things on our onward journey? Encourage everyone to say one thing that they will do or carry into the world. You could mark this by giving each person a tealight candle and inviting them to light it and place it on the table with the cross, Bible, bread and wine.

When everyone has finished, end with the Lord's Prayer and with a spoof announcement at the door as follows:

This is your captain (driver) speaking. We will shortly be arriving at our destination. Thank you for travelling 'Pilgrim Airways' (or whatever you have called your imaginary travel company). We hope you have had a good journey. Please don't forget to take all your belongings with you— everything that God has given to you in this feast. We wish you a safe onward journey to feed and love a hungry and broken world.'

Give everyone a train or plane ticket and then say a final dismissal, either outside the building or facing the outside world.

Go in peace to love and serve the Lord.
In the name of Christ. Amen

——— **Part Three** ———

Food, glorious food!

A six-session course for young communicants

✣

Before you begin

'Food, glorious food!' is a programme intended for children and young people who have been admitted to Holy Communion but have not yet been prepared for confirmation. It could also be used as part of a confirmation preparation programme. It is designed to help children and young people to grow in their understanding of the different aspects of Holy Communion through becoming familiar with the service, what it means in today's world and the practicalities of living out a Christian life each day, at home, at school and with family and friends.

Aims of the course

To continue the nurture programme started with 'Welcome to the Lord's Table' (or other preparation course) by exploring the different sections of the Eucharist. To discuss living out a eucharistic life in the context of home and school and to explore some of the issues in today's world from a Christian perspective.

Themes

Each session is centred upon eating a meal or snack together. The food chosen has a link with the theme of the session and a section of the Eucharist.

- ✪ Ready, steady, cook ....Gathering
- ✪ Healthy eating ....Penitential rite
- ✪ Sweet things ....Gospel

✪ Bring and share the
   needs of the world ....Offertory
✪ Sharing an agape meal ....Holy Communion
✪ Take away pizzas ....Dismissal

Days and times

Sessions could be held after school or on a Friday or Saturday evening. Saturday morning is also a popular time. Equally, it might be possible to meet on a weekday or on Sunday evenings, but the age of the youngest children needs to be taken into account so that they are not having a late night before a school day.

Each session should last for about 90 minutes, but it depends on the size of the group and the type of food being eaten. The outline of each session is based on the following approximate times:

Starters:	15 minutes
Grace or gathering prayer:	2 minutes
Activity:	35 minutes
Main course:	30 minutes
Goodie bag or takeaway:	10 minutes

Any adaptations are noted at the beginning of the particular session.

As the sessions are quite long and have a social as well as a learning aspect, we suggest that they are not held on consecutive weeks. They could be held fortnightly or to correspond with a school term, with three sessions during each half-term. They could also be held during half-term and holidays, maybe as the study part of a 'fun day' with other activities and games included.

Venue

If the group is very small—for example, fewer than six people—meetings could be held in a house. This gives a relaxed family atmosphere and has the advantage of a kitchen designed for preparing and serving meals. Use of the house needs to be considered carefully if it is a family home, however, so that it does not impinge on the needs of the people who live there. It would work best if the house had a second living-room or conservatory. Safety and child protection issues have to be thought out if any meetings with children are held regularly in private houses.

If a church room or hall is used, the needs are different. There should already be safety procedures and insurance in place and the group will probably be the sole user of the premises at the particular time. The challenge is to make the surroundings pleasant and suitable for sharing a meal. Some churches have well-equipped kitchens; others are designed for provision of simple refreshments only. A great deal can be done for very little cost and effort to ensure that the space is warm, the seating and tables are arranged attractively and the walls are clean and decorated with posters.

Whenever possible, try to have tables laid properly before the meeting starts. The children will be making their own place mats in the first session. The practice of eating together at a table is becoming less common in families, so this is an opportunity to reintroduce the social aspect of sharing a meal. Children will also eat more easily and tidily at a table than if they are balancing food on their laps. If there is space, move away from the table for the activities or organize help to clear the plates away quickly. Do not attempt to work or worship in a muddle.

The 'ready box' described in *Welcome to the Lord's Table*[9] could be adapted for use in these sessions.

Leaders and helpers

If the children have recently been prepared for receiving Holy Communion, it is sensible to have some continuity of leadership. The leaders who prepared them will know which parts of the course went well, where further help will be needed and, most importantly, the personalities and needs of the young people. Continuity of leadership does not necessarily mean having exactly the same leaders. One of the leaders who was involved in the preparation could help with the older group or just lead the first two sessions. If that is not practicable, he or she should ideally be involved with the preparation of the course. Putting experienced and new leaders together provides valuable training opportunities as well as ensuring continuity of teaching and forging of relationships between leaders and young people.

Whoever is teaching the course, the clergy should discuss the programme with them, attend planning meetings and provide pastoral and practical support when needed.

However small the group, it is important to maintain the same standards of care and quality of teaching. Any group should always have two adults present, one of whom should be female. Every adult working with children on a regular basis should be approved by the church council and have undergone the Criminal Records Bureau (CRB) enhanced disclosure. This is usually processed by your denominational or diocesan office, who will provide any advice that the church council needs. Further information on choosing and training leaders will be found in *Welcome to the Lord's Table* [10] or will be provided by your denominational or diocesan children's adviser.

Parental involvement

As the children are already part of the church or school community, the parents should have given details about their children and signed consent forms. As each session is based on a meal, however, it is sensible to ask for written information about any allergies or dietary needs the children may have. It is equally important to keep parents informed about what their children will be eating so that they can bear this in mind when preparing other meals. Few things are more infuriating for a parent than to think that their child has had a meal and then find that they only had a snack, or to find that the child has already eaten too much to eat the meal that has been provided.

If any children are new to the church or school, most parents would welcome contact from the leaders. It is a good idea to provide a written programme with names and details of the leaders, and the kind of food that will be provided at each session. Children have remarkably selective memories about dates, times and content of programmes.

The meals

Whatever food is chosen, leaders need to be aware of any children's allergies or dietary needs. As stated above, it is best to ask for this information to be provided on a parental consent form. It is good practice to avoid food and drink with a lot of additives, and to provide a balanced meal whenever possible. In order to put across the teaching point, only a snack is provided in some sessions. As mentioned above, this should be made clear to the parents in advance so that they know whether or not they have to provide a meal for their child after the session.

If children are asked to provide food, please give adequate notice and be sensitive to personal situations. Some families live on very low incomes; others shop only occasionally. There are also issues about providing food that is suitable for every child and the practicalities involved in bringing it to the session if the group meets straight after school. It is probably easier not to ask for contributions on a regular basis.

It is beyond the scope of this book to give advice about food preparation, but it is essential to follow the basic rules of hygiene and safety in the kitchen. Most local authorities provide a basic course on food preparation and hygiene for a nominal sum or free of charge. The kitchen should be generally out of bounds to the children, with firm rules about the number and age of any helpers. It is vital for everyone's health and well-being to insist that everyone washes their hands before preparing or eating food.

Format

Each session follows the same pattern, although the pattern may vary according to the size of the group. Some parts of the session will overlap each other. For example, the general conversation during the meal may turn into the beginning of the teaching session. If the group is very small, there may be no need for an assembling activity as everyone will be involved in collecting food. The basic format is as follows:

- ✪ Ice breaker or assembling activity while food is prepared, collected or served
- ✪ Prayer or grace
- ✪ Eating and socializing
- ✪ Teaching and discussion
- ✪ Activities
- ✪ Focus on the world (on Monday morning, how do we apply what we have learnt?)
- ✪ Worship (loosely linked to the relevant section of the Eucharist)
- ✪ Plans for the next meeting

Gathering

Ready, steady, cook!

Aim
To understand that all sorts of people gather for Holy Communion as part of God's family. Each person is different. We need each other and we need to understand each other better.

Food and resources

You will need:

- Either ready-produced smoothies or a selection of fruit such as bananas, strawberries, apples, blackberries and so on, and a smoothie maker or blender. A variety of smoothies are available in most supermarkets and health food shops
- Pictures of fruits
- Meat and vegetable burgers, bread rolls, hot dogs, onions, ketchup and relish
- Cheese
- Copies of the 'Body of Christ' place mat (see Appendix Two, page 164)
- Copies of the body parts templates (see Appendix Two, pages 165 and 166)
- Felt-tipped pens

⊙ If possible, a laminator (one can often can be borrowed from a local school or youth centre)
⊙ Small paper or plastic goodie bags containing fruit and a cardboard 'body' (see Appendix Two, page 167)

The menu

Fruit smoothies
Meat or vegetable burgers
Hot dogs
Bread rolls
Garnishes: cheese, onions, ketchup and so on

Starters

As each child arrives, offer him or her a smoothie drink. As this is the first meeting, welcome each person individually and allow time for the group to introduce themselves to each other. Do not assume that everyone knows everyone else. Invite them to talk in pairs about things that are nothing to do with church—home, family, school, interests and so on—while the group assembles.

Have laid out either a selection of fruits, including those used in the smoothie (up to three of each kind, depending on the size of the group), or pictures cut out from food magazines or downloaded from the Internet. Invite the children to decide, in groups of two or three, which fruits are in their smoothie.

Gather everyone and ask them to say what they thought was in the smoothie, then give the answer. Explain that smoothies are made by gathering and mixing fruits together. At the start of the service, we gather, not as different fruits but as different people.

Gathering prayer

Say this grace or gathering prayer together.

Loving Lord, thank you that you made us all different and have gathered us here together. Thank you that we all bring something special and different as members of your family. Help us to appreciate each other more today. Amen

Activity

Read 1 Corinthians 12:12–14, 18 and 20–26. Give each child a copy of the 'Body of Christ' place mat. Invite them to decorate and then ask the leaders to laminate it. (See page 164 for a template.)

Invite each child to choose one of the selection of body parts from the template on pages 165 and 166. (Depending on the size of your group, you might need more than one template.) Ask them in turn what is useful and important about each of the body parts: for example, 'I am a leg/a hand/a head. You need me because…'

Next, ask everyone to find someone with another part of the body, which they need to be attached to. For example, the hand will need to find the arm, the foot will need to find the leg, the leg will need to find the body and so on. Once everyone is attached, ask everyone to go round and say, 'A foot needs a leg because…'

Explain that the Bible talks about Christians being like a body because we are all different but we all need each other. Being part of the family and coming together for a service of Holy Communion reminds us that we belong together as the body of Christ.

Main course

When we meet for Holy Communion, we gather for a meal. Jesus is the most important guest at our meal, but he is also the one who serves us. We will find out more about this in the next few sessions.

At this point, the leader needs to become the waiter. (You might like to dress up in bow tie or apron, with a cloth over your arm.) The leader takes orders from everyone. Each person can choose either a meat or veggie burger or a hot dog, and then choose the garnish: onions, cheese, relish or ketchup.

Serve everyone with his or her food. At the end of the meal, remind people that lots of different things go to make up a burger or a hot dog: you need bread, meat or vegetables, and onions. Everything goes together to make up the taste. In a service of Holy Communion, we have lots of different things to make up this very special family meal.

Goodie bags

Give each child a bag containing a piece of fruit to remind them of the smoothie, and a cardboard 'body'.

Challenge for the next session

Give each child a note with the information about the next session and a reminder to bring back their place mats.

Prayer

Finish by saying the following prayer. This is best said by the leader line by line, with the children and helpers repeating each line back.

Loving Lord Jesus,
Thank you that we are all different.
Thank you that we need each other.
Thank you that you are the special guest at Holy Communion.
Help us to feed on you and enjoy you and each other more. Amen

Penitential rite

Healthy eating

Aim

To help us understand that we make choices every day. Each choice we make has a consequence for ourselves and for other people. Some choices are good, but some are harmful and damage our relationship with God and each other.

The theme of this session is based on the words from the confession in the Book of Common Prayer: 'We have left undone those things which we ought to have done and we have done those things which we ought not to have done.' To paraphrase this in food language, we might say, 'We have eaten too many things that are not good for us and we have not eaten things that will help us to grow healthily.'

Food and resources

You will need:

⊙ Two tables of food set on either side of the room. One table has healthy food such as fruit, vegetables, wholemeal bread, seeds and water. The other has junk food such as crisps, boiled sweets and fizzy drinks

⊙ A 'Ten healthy choices' game board for each child (see Appendix Two, page 168)

- A counter for each child
- A copy of the 'Choices' questions (see pp. 128–130)
- Food such as that listed in the menu
- Paper or plastic goodie bags containing small bars of soap

The menu

A mini buffet of attractive and healthy food such as salad, fruit, nuts, seeds, squares of cheese, egg, wholemeal bread, fruit juice and water.

Starters

Invite the group, as they arrive, to choose a couple of items from the tables as a snack to start the session. After a few minutes, gather the group together and talk about why they have chosen that particular food. Make the point that none of the foods are very bad, but if we eat only unhealthy foods and don't choose good foods, then we will become unhealthy. We will not grow very well and we will lack energy. Next, ask the group which is the most important thing on both of the tables. (*Water—because nothing can live without it.*)

Gathering prayer

Say the following gathering prayer together.

Loving Lord, thank you for gathering us together again. Help us to understand more about the choices we can make. Teach us to make good choices for you as we pray and play together. Amen

Activities

Play a game of 'Ten healthy choices'. This game is similar to 'Snakes and Ladders', but is not intended to be competitive. Each player has a board and a counter. The leader reads out a question, and the players decide which of the two or three options they would take. The leader then directs the players to move their counters forwards or backwards according to their choice of answer.

Ten healthy choices

1. For breakfast, will you choose to drink milk, fizzy lemonade or fruit juice?

   Milk ....Go forward 2
   Fizzy lemonade ....Go back 2
   Fruit juice ....Go forward 2

2. You are going to a football match. It is a cold day and the forecast is for rain. Do you go out in your football T-shirt or do you add a jacket and a football scarf?

   Wear just a T-shirt ....Go back 2
   Add a jacket and scarf............................Go forward 4

3. You are buying your school lunch. You have enough money for an apple or a chocolate bar. Which do you choose?

   Apple ....Go forward 4
   Chocolate bar ....Go back 4

4. You are hot and thirsty. Do you choose to suck a lollipop, have a drink of water or drink a can of Coke?

Lollipop ....Go back 4
Coke ....Go back 2
Water ....Go forward 6

5. You are going to a disco and everyone seems to have nicer clothes than you. You can't afford to buy something new. Do you go in the clothes you have, ask a friend if you can borrow something, or take a cool top from a shop without paying?

Go in what you have...Go forward 6
Borrow something...Go forward 2
Take top without paying ....Go back 6

6. You borrow a CD from a friend and accidentally damage it. Do you hand it back without saying anything, own up and say you are sorry, or own up and offer to buy another one when you have the money?

Say nothing ....Go back 5
Apologize ....Go forward 3
Offer to replace it ....Go forward 5

7. Someone in your class has the latest computer game. Do you choose to bully them until they give it to you, ask if you can have a turn, or decide to save up for your own?

Bully them...Go back 6
Ask for a turn ....Go forward 6
Decide to save up ....Go forward 6

8. Somebody makes fun of you because you go to church. Do you stop going, say you agree that it's naff but your parents make you go, hit the other person, or say that church is OK and invite him or her along?

Stop going..Go back 6
Say it is naff ....Stay put (it might be true!)
Hit the other person ....Go back 6
Invite him or her along ....Go forward 6

9. An elderly woman falls over in the street. Do you see if you can help her or do you laugh and run away?

See if she is all right ....Go forward 4
Run away ....Go back 4

10. Somebody has been very unkind to you. Do you feel hurt but try to forget it, make rude comments every time you see the other person, or imagine dark revenge but actually do nothing?

Try to forget it..Go forward 6
Make rude comments ....Go back 6
Imagine revenge but do nothing ....Stay put

When you have finished, remind the children that the game was about choosing. We make choices all the time. Some of our choices concern things such as what to eat that will help us to stay healthy. Some are about the way we behave towards God and other people—whether we choose to do what is right or what is wrong.

Zacchaeus' five healthy choices

Read Luke 19:1–10. Together with the children, look at the choices that Zacchaeus made and the consequences of his actions.

✪ Climbed the tree because he wanted to see Jesus (seeking)
✪ Accepted Jesus' invitation for hospitality (responding)
✪ Recognized that he had made bad choices (contrition)

- ☼ Confessed his wrong choices publicly and offered to put things right (restitution)
- ☼ Jesus was thrilled that Zacchaeus had chosen the right way of living (restoration)

Explain to the group that we are constantly faced with choices and that there are consequences to the choices we make. Zacchaeus made a choice that changed his way of living, and he was much happier for it.

Before we meet Jesus in his word and sacrament, we need to remember the things that we have done wrong and ask for his forgiveness. One symbol of repentance and the new life it brings is water. We are forgiven and given a fresh start, not because we deserve it but because God is gracious in his love for us. One of the things we can do as a symbol that we are sorry for what we have done wrong is to wash our hands.

Grace

Say the following grace together. Have ready a bowl of warm water, some soap and a clean towel.

Loving Lord, we are sorry for making the wrong choices sometimes. Please wash us clean and help us to choose well so that we can be the people you want us to be. Amen

Ask the children to wash their hands—in silence, if possible. Then pray again.

Thank you for washing us clean. Thank you for giving us a fresh start and thank you for this fresh food you give to us to eat. Amen

Main course

Ask everyone to lay the table and put out their own place mats. Next, invite everyone to choose five items from the healthy food section. Talk about how these different foods make us healthy. Then explain that the better we eat, the more energy we have to live better lives: good food in equals good stuff out! Encourage the children to eat more than five things if they wish, so that food is not wasted.

Goodie bags

Give everyone a small bar of soap to take home with them as a reminder that we need to wash regularly to stay clean, but we still have the choice. Talk about what might happen if we don't wash our hands regularly.

Challenge for the next session

As the children have just eaten five healthy things, ask them to write down five things that would make their life and the lives of those around them better, such as helping to keep their bedrooms tidy, being nice to people at school, speaking the truth and so on.

Tell everyone about the next session, for which they will need a sweet tooth!

Prayer

Loving Lord, thank you for all that we have learnt today and all that we have eaten today. Thank you that choosing you means choosing the healthy option. As we go from here, help us to live more healthy lives and make good and healthy choices. Amen

Gospel

Sweet things

Aim

To show that (for Christians) the Bible is like good food: we need it each day. Reading and understanding the Bible—the sweet words of God—is both good for us and enjoyable. One of the psalmists wrote, 'How sweet are your words to my taste, sweeter than honey to my mouth' (Psalm 119:103, NIV).

Food and resources

You will need:

- A large bar of good-quality chocolate
- A plate, knife and fork
- A pair of gloves, a scarf and a hat
- A large dice (foam dice are available from some educational shops, or you can make one out of a tissue box)
- A chocolate fountain or chocolate melted in a bowl over a saucepan
- Fruit and marshmallows to dip into the chocolate
- A fork for each member of the group
- Bibs and napkins
- 'Bible quote' exercise on cards or sheets of paper
- Pens or pencils

> ❁ Paper or plastic goodie bags containing a card with the Bible verse written on it and a small bar of Fair Trade chocolate

The menu

Fruit and sweets dipped into chocolate.

Starters

Get all the children into a circle and place the chocolate bar on a plate with the knife and fork in the middle. Put the scarf, hat and gloves beside it. Pass the dice round the circle and throw it in turn. When someone throws a six, he or she comes into the centre, puts on the scarf, hat and gloves, and carves the chocolate, eating as much as possible. Meanwhile, everyone else is still throwing the dice. When the next person throws a six, he or she takes over.

Gathering prayer

Say the following gathering prayer together.

Loving Lord, thank you for the food we eat and for the sweet things that we enjoy. Thank you also for your word. Help us to discover more about its sweetness in our lives today. Amen

Activity

Photocopy and cut out the selection of Bible quotations about food (see below) and place them on a table. Invite people to fill in the gaps with the name of the food that they think fits there. Then look up the Bible reference to find the answers, which, for the purposes of this book, are taken from the Contemporary English Version.

'I am the _____ that gives life! No one who comes to me will ever be hungry. No one who has faith in me will ever be thirsty' (John 6:35).

Jesus took some _____ in his hands and gave thanks for it. He broke the _____ and handed it to his apostles. Then he said, 'This is my body, which is given for you. Eat this as a way of remembering me!' (Luke 22:19).

When the disciples got out of the boat, they saw some _____ and a charcoal fire with _____ on it (John 21:9).

'We have only five small loaves of _____ and two _____. If we are going to feed all these people, we will have to go and buy food' (Luke 9:13).

One time the Philistines brought their army together to destroy a crop of _____ growing in a field near Lehi (2 Samuel 23:11).

If you are thirsty, come and drink _____! If you don't have any money, come, eat what you want! Drink _____ and _____ without paying a penny (Isaiah 55:1).

If Benjamin must go with you, take the governor a gift of some of the best things from our own country, such as perfume, _____, _____, _____ _____, and _____ (Genesis 43:11).

Reproduced with permission from *Creative Communion* published by BRF 2008 (978 1 84101 533 0) www.barnabasinchurches.org.uk

The woman replied, 'Sir, please give me a drink of that ___ !
Then I won't get thirsty and have to come to this well again'
(John 4:15).

But it must be done in the second month, in the evening of
the fourteenth day. Eat the Passover _____ with thin _____
and bitter _____ (Numbers 9:11).

Here's one last one for fun! Can the children guess the different
foods here from the book of Numbers?

In Egypt we could eat all the _____ we wanted, and there
were _____ , _____ , _____ , and _____ (Numbers
11:5).

Look up the answers together, and then go back to the quotation,
'I am the bread that gives life!' (John 6:35). Explain that the Bible
is like bread. It is essential for the proper growth and spiritual
development of Christians. Just as food is necessary for the body, so
God's word is essential for the soul. We need a proper spiritual diet
to grow spiritually. It is possible to grow physically without God's
word, but we will not grow spiritually. That is why many people read
small bite-sized pieces of the Bible each day as part of their daily
spiritual meal. You might want to encourage the older children to try
to read the Bible regularly.

Main course

Show the children the chocolate fountain (or the chocolate melted
in a bowl over a saucepan). The chocolate fountain is full of melted
chocolate. It is heated up in the machine, but what would happen

if we unplugged it? It would stop flowing. The chocolate would set, crystallize and become impossible to stir and use. (Equally, when we take the chocolate melted over a saucepan away from the heat source, it starts to set, crystallize and become impossible to stir and use.)

In the same way, we need to be plugged into the word of God. Ask the children where, in the chocolate fountain, the chocolate is coming from. Is it being magically created or is it the same chocolate going round and round? Explain that, like the chocolate, the same piece of the Bible can help us at different times. We need to keep reading it because it is like a fountain, and we will find out new things each time we read it.

NB: If you are using chocolate that has been heated over a saucepan, you will need to stir it to heat it evenly and stop it sticking. This is not such a good illustration but still shows that the same chocolate appears at different times and places.

In Psalm 1:1–3, people who love the word of God are likened to trees growing beside a flowing stream—trees that produce fruit in season and always have leaves. In the New Testament, the writer of the book of Hebrews likens the Bible to a sharp sword: 'What God has said isn't only alive and active! It is sharper than any double-edged sword. His word can cut through our spirits and souls and through our joints and marrow, until it discovers the desires and thoughts of our hearts' (Hebrews 4:12). So we can see that the Bible is more than just a book: it is living and active; it helps us to grow and makes us strong and healthy, like a tree growing beside a stream and drawing its sustenance from the flowing water. Also, when we read the Bible, it seeks out our deepest thoughts in the same way that a sword can cut through the hardest materials.

Now bring out the fruit and marshmallows and allow the group to dip items of their choice into the chocolate and enjoy them. **NB:** If you are melting chocolate over a saucepan, it is important to remove the pan from the heat and supervise this activity very carefully, as chocolate burns are very unpleasant.

Goodie bags

Give everyone a goodie bag containing a small bar of Fair Trade chocolate and this Bible verse printed on a card, which the children can decorate: 'God's word can cut through our spirits and souls... until it discovers the desires and thoughts of our hearts' (Hebrews 4:12).

Challenge for the next session

Ask the children to bring to the next session an item of Fair Trade food, or some fresh food that has come from abroad. Ask them to keep the label that shows its country of origin. (As well as the usual shops and Traidcraft outlets, they could try Oxfam for a wide selection of dried fruits and seeds.)

Prayer

Loving Lord, thank you for feeding us not just with food in our mouths but with words from your mouth, in the Bible. Help us to keep reading and to understand more of your stories of love and purpose for us. Amen

Offertory

Bring and share the needs of the world

Aim

To help the children to connect with the rest of the world. To remind them that our food comes from all over the world, and that Jesus came not just for us but also for the whole world.

Food and resources

You will need:

⚙ A large map of the world that can be placed on a table or the floor. Use a large atlas or see if you can borrow a map from a school or buy one at an educational shop.

⚙ Food items, preferably fairly traded, from unusual countries, brought in by the children themselves.

⚙ Ingredients for one or more of the Fair Trade recipes (see 'Main course' below)

⚙ Paper or plastic goodie bags containing Fair Trade information, a recipe card, a copy of a small map of the world or globe ball, and a prayer card (see instructions on page 145 and the template on page 169)

The menu

The food for this session is a simple meal made from typical Fair Traded ingredients, together with a dish created from the various contributions that the children have brought.

Starters

Invite each person who has brought some food from a different part of the world to tell everyone which country it is from and then place it on the map. You may need to help the children with this, for some of the less well-known countries. Include your own items if anyone has forgotten theirs and to add to the variety.

Gathering prayer

Say the following gathering prayer together.

Loving Lord, it is good to be together again as your family. Help us today to think not just about each other but also about the world that you love so much and people who have different and more difficult lives than we do. Amen

Activity

Talk briefly about different growing conditions and how people live in the various countries that provide our food. You will find details from websites such as www.globalgang.org.uk, www.tearfund.org.uk and www.cafod.org.uk/resources.

Explain that sharing Holy Communion is about sharing the needs of the wider world and not just our own needs. Most people in this country have plenty of food to eat, but today there are many countries where there is not enough food to eat or to share with other people. Intercession brings the whole world into our worship. We ask God not just to feed us but also to use us to feed the wider world and make it a fairer place. Talk about the different conditions of food in the world. We depend on all parts of the world for our food, so we need to pray for them.

Now make up a recipe using the ingredients that are on the map, and nothing else. Ask the children to work in pairs to think about what they might make. They can include all or just a few of the ingredients. When they have finished discussing and planning their recipe, ask them to share their ideas with the rest of the group.

Read John 6:32–36. Jesus said, 'I am the bread that gives life! No one who comes to me will ever be hungry. No one who has faith in me will ever be thirsty' (v. 35). Ask the children what they eat more of than anything else. Ask them to write a list of the five things they eat the most, starting with the biggest amount. Is bread on the list? If so, where is it on the list? How many of the children ever go a single day without eating bread in some form (anything from a bread roll or toast to pizza or a burger bun). Ask if they can imagine not having bread. In China, people don't eat bread very often, so they don't understand the significance of Jesus saying, 'I am the bread that gives life!' Instead, the Chinese Bible says, 'I am the rice that gives life!' because in that country rice is the staple diet, just as bread is here.

Every day we eat different food from around the world. When we are eating in church, we need to remember that some people don't eat the same food, have the same things, or live their lives in the same way as we do. We need to pray for people in different parts of the world, for their lives, their food and their situations.

Ask the children to look again at the food they have brought and the recipes they have planned. Together, pray for all the different countries represented by the foods they have brought. Go back to the map and pray for the food growers in those countries—for example, the bean growers in Kenya, apple growers in New Zealand, rice growers in Asia, mango growers in the West Indies, coffee growers in Rwanda and so on.

Dear Lord, thank you for all the food we have from your world. Today we pray especially for...

Main course

This part of the meal will be based on the staple diet of a Developing World country. If you have a congregation member or a friend with first-hand knowledge, see if they can provide or suggest a simple meal. If that is not possible, there are a few books of recipes from different parts of the world that are designed for children and young people.[11] Be aware that many children are very conservative about food and may be reluctant to taste something strange or try food that contains hot spices. The following receipe suggestions will give a basic meal that most children should enjoy eating.

Fennel and orange salad

This kind of salad is commonly served as a starter in Morocco.

You will need:
- Two small-leafed lettuces broken into separate leaves
- Two medium fennel bulbs and two carrots
- Two large oranges
- Flat leaf parsley to garnish

For the dressing, you will need:
- Orange juice
- Two tbsp lemon juice
- Four tsp orange juice
- Two tsp honey
- Two tbsp olive oil
- Salt to taste

Wash and break up the lettuces; thinly slice the fennel and oranges, and grate the carrots. Layer them on a large plate. Combine the dressing ingredients, pour the dressing over the salad and garnish with chopped parsley. Serve chilled. This salad could be served with hard-boiled eggs, cheese and pitta bread.

Pineapple and cinnamon crumble squares

This recipe can be made with fresh pineapple, but a tin of crushed pineapple is equally acceptable and will avoid the need for sharp knives.

You will need:
- ❂ One tin of crushed pineapple
- ❂ 50g caster sugar
- ❂ One tsp ground cinnamon
- ❂ 200g self-raising flour
- ❂ 250g soft light brown sugar
- ❂ 150g rolled oats
- ❂ 150g butter

Drain the fruit and place it in a saucepan with the caster sugar and cinnamon. Cook on a low heat for 15 minutes, stirring occasionally. As the pineapple softens, break it up and continue to cook until it is very soft.

Lightly grease a 20.5cm square cake tin and line with baking parchment. Mix together the flour, brown sugar and rolled oats. Melt the butter in a pan and add to the dry ingredients. Spread half the crumble mixture on the bottom of the cake tin and press down. Pour the pineapple mixture over the crumble layer. Sprinkle over the remaining crumble mixture and press down lightly.

Bake in a preheated over at 190°C/Gas Mark 5 for 30–35

minutes. Remove from the oven and mark out the squares with a knife, but allow them to cool before removing them from the tin. Eat warm or cold.

Fresh hummous

You will need:
- One tin of chickpeas
- Tahini paste
- Lemon juice
- Olive oil
- Greek yoghurt

Drain the chickpeas and put them into a food processor. Add one spoonful of tahini paste (optional) together with the juice from one lemon and a healthy glug of olive oil. Season lightly with salt and pepper. Blitz this mixture into a pulp and then add the Greek yoghurt and olive oil to moisten the paste. Blitz again and serve with raw carrots, pitta bread or crackers.

Raita dip

Children will enjoy dunking crackers or pitta bread into this simple dip.

You will need:
- Half a cucumber, finely diced
- One pot of Greek natural yoghurt
- Fresh or dried mint

Dice the cucumber into very small pieces, and mix with yoghurt and mint. Supply broken crackers or strips of pitta bread for the children to dunk into the dip.

After thinking about prayers for the world and having a meal together, move on to think about what we mean by the term 'offertory'. Offering is about offering to God: it is not about taking a collection or really about money at all, but about how we can give more of ourselves to God. God wants to use us to help build a better world and better homes. That means offering something of who we are and the things we are good at to God—because all our gifts come from God.

Prayer cards

Make up prayer cards for the children to use over the course of the coming week (and beyond). Either give the children pieces of heavyweight card to decorate and write out their own wording, or have the cards ready made, so that all the children need to do is decorate them.

Lord God, I offer to you everything I am and everything I do. Especially today, I want to give............ Help me this week to give my best to you.

Goodie bags

Give each child a goodie bag containing Fair Trade information, a recipe card or instructions on how to make the food the children have just eaten, a copy of a map of the world and the prayer card they made during the session. Talk about the things that we can offer to God. In what ways can we help others? Talk about things such as not wasting our food, praying for the people who grow our food, contributing to a harvest festival and so on.

NB: Fair Trade information can be obtained from websites such as those listed on page 140. A copy of a map of the world can be obtained via schools or educational suppliers, or through your local school contact.

Challenge for the next session

Ask the children to fill in their prayer cards during the week and remember to bring them back next time. For the next session, you may wish to give script cards with the words for the *Seder* ceremony to the children who are going to speak them, so that they can read them through before the next session. (See Appendix Two, page 170, for individual script cards.)

Prayer

Finish the session with the following prayer.

Blessed are you Lord, God of all creation. In thanks for your goodness, we offer ourselves; people of faith, made by your hands. Take us and use us for your own. Amen

Holy Communion

Sharing an agape meal

Aim

To help the children to understand the origins of the Last Supper and the connection between Passover and Holy Communion.

Outline and suggested timing

This session is almost entirely taken up with a meal based on the Jewish Passover meal, the *Seder*, so the format is different from the other five sessions in this programme. The suggested outline and timing is as follows.

Starters:	20 minutes
Gathering prayer:	2 minutes
Main course:	70 minutes

Food and resources

You will need:

- ☀ A white tablecloth
- ☀ Candles
- ☀ Bread mix for the tear-and-share bread

- A little flour
- Baking trays
- Horseradish sauce (extra hot)
- Fresh parsley
- Small pieces of cooked lamb
- Small glasses of 'wine' (grape juice)
- Matzoh crackers (for example, Rausken's)
- Grapes
- Cards containing each child's words for the *Seder*
- Paper or plastic goodie bags containing a candle, a matzoh cracker, a radish (a salad one will be fine), a picture of a lamb, a bread roll and a small carton of red fruit juice

The menu

Bread; lamb; bitter herbs; matzoh crackers; grapes; grape juice

Starters

Preheat the oven to the temperature indicated on the bread mix packet and have some bread mixture ready made for making bread plaits. Make sure all the children and adults have washed their hands. Then give each child three pieces of dough to plait together to make a 'tear-and-share' piece of bread. Bake the bread in the oven according to the instructions on the bread mix packet.

While the bread is baking, ask the children to help to set up the table. The table is to be set for a simplified Jewish *Seder* meal. The meal is not a re-enactment of a *Seder*; it is meant just to illustrate and help the children to imagine what Jesus was doing during the Passover meal on the last night of his life on earth.

Ask the children to lay the table with a white tablecloth, some candles, horseradish, chopped parsley and small pieces of cooked lamb. Place these items along the table. There is no need for plates and knives. Invite everyone to gather round the table.

You will then need to give everyone who has a speaking part their lines written out on a piece of paper. Cue each child in as you come to his or her part. Invite everyone else to listen and be caught up in the drama of the story. Explain that, at moments during the story, there is a response that everyone makes. Practise the bidding, 'We praise you, Lord, king of life' and encourage everyone else to respond enthusiastically.

For this simplified version of a *Seder* meal, you will need an adult who reads well to take the part of the father. The children will take the parts of the mother and the four children. If the group is very small, the parts can be doubled up.

Gathering prayer

Begin by saying the following gathering prayer together.

Blessed are you Lord, God of all creation. You have given us food to eat and friends to share it with. We thank you for the story of your love for us and for all your people. Bless us as we share this food together and hear the story of Jesus' love for us. Amen

Main course

Father: Jewish people have celebrated the special Passover meal for thousands of years. When they celebrate this meal, they remember that God delivered them from slavery in Egypt and that death passed over their doors because they followed God's commands. On the night before Jesus died, he was with his friends (the disciples) in an upper room celebrating the Passover. Jesus chose the Passover meal as the basis for what Christians now celebrate as Holy Communion (or the Eucharist). God cared for his people long ago and cares for us today. Today we are going to be able to see, hear and taste the great love that God has for us.

The mother of the house, *(name)*, will now light the candles. As she does this, let's be quiet and pray that God will help to bring the special meaning of Passover to each one of us.

Mother: *(Lighting the candles)* Blessed are you, O Lord our God, king of the universe. You have chosen each one of us, and made us holy. In your name we light these lights. Blessed be God for ever!

Father: When people gather for the Passover meal, they remember all that God had done for them in bringing them out of Egypt and freeing them from slavery.

Youngest child: Why is this meal different? Why do we only eat unleavened bread on this night?

Father: On this night we eat matzoh, unleavened bread, to remind us of the time when the Jewish people were in slavery in Egypt. On the night when they left their houses, they had no time to let their bread rise and bake it. They took raw dough on their journey and baked it in the hot desert sun into hard crackers called matzoh.

(Breaking the crackers in two) We also remember that Jesus' body was broken. We save the other half of the matzoh cracker for the end of the meal.

We wrap it and hide it—just as Jesus' body was wrapped and laid in a tomb.

Children, close your eyes as I hide the matzoh cracker somewhere in the room! *(The children close their eyes and the leader hides the cracker)* Now, in remembrance that Jesus blessed the bread at the Last Supper, we, too, bless this bread.

We praise you, Lord, king of life.

All: We praise you, Lord, king of life.

The leader passes round the matzoh cracker and invites everyone to break off a piece and eat it. They also need to retain a piece of matzoh for the bitter herbs.

Child 2: Why do we eat only bitter herbs on this night?

Father: On other nights of the week, we eat vegetables of all kinds, but at Passover we eat bitter herbs to remember how bitter life was for the Israelites in Egypt under the cruel Pharaoh.

Scoop up a bit of the horseradish sauce on your matzoh and smell it. Sometimes it can bring tears to your eyes. Remember those who were in slavery thousands of years ago and who are still in slavery today. Remember their tears. Taste some if you want, but be careful—it's spicy and hot!

We praise you, Lord, king of life.

All: We praise you, Lord, king of life.

Child 3: Why do we eat standing up?

Father: We eat standing up because the Israelites were told to eat the Passover meal quickly, their coats at the ready and sandals on their feet, ready to leave Egypt.

Child 4: Why do we eat lamb?

Father: We eat lamb because God told Moses to choose a perfect lamb to eat. Some of the blood of the lamb was to be put on the doorposts of each house. The lamb was to be roasted and eaten with bitter herbs and thin bread made without yeast. The people were to eat quickly and be ready to travel. This meal was the Passover feast in honour of the Lord God. When God passed through Egypt, he would see the blood on the door of the houses and the people would not be harmed. This story is told in Exodus 12:3–13. We remember that it is God who brought our ancestors out of slavery.

Child 5: Why is Jesus called the Lamb of God?

Father: Jesus is called the Lamb of God because he was perfect like the lamb in the story of Moses. No more lambs need to be sacrificed to honour God because Jesus has died for each one of us and taken away the sin of the world.

We praise you, Lord, king of life.

All: We praise you, Lord, king of life.

Father: It is time to share the hidden matzoh. Can anyone find it? When you have found it, bring it back here and we will share it. This bread was hidden and now it is back. It reminds us that when we share bread and wine we celebrate Jesus' death, but that he has also risen from the dead and is alive for ever.

We praise you, Lord, king of life.

All: We praise you, Lord, king of life.

Father: It was at this point in the last supper that Jesus added in the words, 'This is my body, which is given for you. Eat this as a way of remembering

Reproduced with permission from *Creative Communion* published by BRF 2008 (978 1 84101 533 0) www.barnabasinchurches.org.uk

me!' Then Jesus passed the bread round to his disciples just as we are going to do now.

Pause while the matzoh crackers are passed round the group.

Father: And now the juice from the grape. The cup of wine at the Passover meal usually symbolized Elijah and waiting for God's anointed one—the Messiah. But Jesus is God's Messiah. He has come! When Jesus took the cup at the Last Supper, he said that the wine represented his blood, which was poured out for our sins.

We praise you, Lord, king of life.

All: We praise you, Lord, king of life.

Father: Now we all share the cup of juice.

At this point, the children share the juice from a single goblet, or drink from their own glasses.

Father: Finally, we raise our cups as if we were giving someone three cheers. Give thanks to the Lord, for he is good!

All: Give thanks to the Lord, for he is good!

Father: Give thanks to the Lord, God of all creation!

All: Give thanks to the Lord, God of all creation!

Father: Give thanks to him who saved Israel from slavery!

All: Give thanks to him who saved Israel from slavery!

Father: Give thanks to the Lord who has saved us and given us life!

All: Give thanks to the Lord who has saved us and given us life!

✛

Ask the children what they liked the most about this special meal. You might want to have a mini-quiz to remind them of what each item symbolized in the story. Items include the candles, the matzoh, the bitter herbs, the lamb, the bread and the 'wine' (juice).

By now, the plaited bread should be cooked. Bring the bread in with some grapes and pass the food round like a 'tear-and-share' loaf. Explain that bread and grapes are what we share at Holy Communion. This time, instead of coming to the front of the church, we will gather round and pass the food to each other.

Goodie bags

Give each child a goodie bag to take home, containing a candle, a matzoh cracker, a radish, a picture of a lamb, a bread roll and a small carton of red fruit juice.

Challenge for the next session

Invite the children to write a 'thank you' letter for the meal that God has given to them. The next and final session is a bit like a farewell party. Ask everyone to bring the pizza toppings of their choice. They can bring anything, but it needs to be enough for themselves and one other person. That way, there will be plenty to go round.

Prayer

Loving Lord, thank you for everything you have fed us with today. You have fed us through sharing your story, the story of your people and yourself. Thank you for bread and wine. Help us to treasure this food, which is now in us, and to enjoy and remember you each day. Amen

6

Dismissal

Takeaway pizzas

Aim
To help the children to understand that as well as 'eating in'—
gathering round the Lord's table and sharing together—we are
also sent out, to 'take away' and share the love of God with our
friends and the wider world.

Food and resources

You will need:
- Pizza bases, tomato sauce base mix, and various pizza
  toppings provided by the children
- Baking trays and a slice
- Large (A3) sheets of paper
- Pens and coloured pencils
- Heavyweight cardboard
- Split-pin fasteners
- Scissors and rulers
- Paper or plastic goodie bags, which may contain a grace
  cube or card (see Appendix Two, page 172), a chocolate bar,
  a piece of fruit and a small bottle of water
- Red paper to make heart-shaped invitations

The menu

Pizza with various toppings.

Starters

Imagine that your church is a takeaway pizza or food restaurant, and you have to design a poster or TV advert for it. Start with something like, '(Name of your church)—the best eat-in and takeaway place in town'. What would you like to say about what people can receive in church and what you want to share with people about your church? If you have time, you might even like to make up a jingle or slogan.

Gathering prayer

Say the following gathering prayer together.

Generous God, we thank you for all the food and the love that you give us through communion with you. Help us today to feast on you, but also to share with you and to feed a hungry world with the love we enjoy today. Amen

Activity

Read Acts 2:43–47. Ask the children to pick out the things that this group of Christians did. The list will include:

- ✪ Gathering together
- ✪ Selling their possessions
- ✪ Distributing to those in need
- ✪ Eating together happily and freely

Explain to the children that this was how the early Church used to live. Are things different now? Do we do any of the things or similar things to those in the reading? Then ask the children to work out six actions that Christians should do, not in the church building but among friends and neighbours, at school and at home. How can we take the love of God into the world today, as the early Christians did?

Pizza wheels

Ask the group to make cardboard pizzas. Cut out two circles with a 15–20cm diameter. Using a ruler, divide both circles into sixths. In one of the circles, cut out a segment the size of one-sixth of the circle (see diagram on page 171). In each of the six sections of the other circle, draw and colour images of the different things that the church should and could be doing out in the world. If anyone does not enjoy drawing, they could write about the things instead.

Then place the two cards one on top of the other, the card with the missing segment on top. Ask an adult to make a hole in the middle of the two cards with a sharp point (a sharp knife or pair of compasses will do) and fix them together with a split-pin fastener.

When the children have completed their cardboard pizzas, gather the whole group together and invite each child to present their pizza wheel to someone else. This person moves the wheel with the missing segment round 'slice by slice' and talks about how they want to be the church in the world and about the things they are going to take away from sharing Holy Communion with each other.

Main course

Spend some time making pizzas with the various toppings. The pizzas should be of the size that can be shared between two people, so ask the children to work in pairs to decide which toppings they would like on their pizza. If space is limited, invite two children at a time to make their pizza while everyone else is designing an invitation heart for a forthcoming church event.

For the invitations, ask the children to cut heart shapes out of red paper. Add the words:

Dear .... you are invited to come with me to......... at .... on .... I would love it if you would come.

Put the completed heart invitations in the child's goodie bag.

As the children are making their pizzas, remind them that they brought enough food for two. Ask them who they would most want to share some food with today, and who they would like to invite to the next Holy Communion service at church.

Once all the pizzas are prepared, they can be cooked in time to be eaten before the end of the session.

Goodie bags

As this is the last session, you might want to put a few treats in the bag to remind the children of everything they have done in these sessions. The treats could include a grace cube or card (see Appendix Two, page 172), a chocolate bar, a piece of fruit and a small bottle of water.

Prayer

Finish with the following prayer.

Lord, we thank you for feeding us. We thank you that we have shared your word and your food. Help us to carry this into the world and share it as you did. Help us to live as you want us to live and to show and invite others to do the same. Amen

Go in peace to love and serve the Lord.
In the name of Christ! Amen

✤

Eucharistic Prayer H

Leader: The Lord be with you *(or)* The Lord is here.
All: And also with you. *(or)* His Spirit is with us.
Leader: Lift up your hearts.
All: We lift them to the Lord.
Leader: Let us give thanks to the Lord our God.
All: It is right to give thanks and praise.
Leader: It is right to praise you, Father, Lord of all creation; in your love you made us for yourself. When we turned away you did not reject us, but came to meet us in your Son.
All: You embraced us as your children and welcomed us to sit and eat with you.
Leader: In Christ you shared our life that we might live in him and he in us.
All: He opened his arms of love upon the cross and made for all the perfect sacrifice for sin.
Leader: On the night he was betrayed, at supper with his friends he took bread, and gave you thanks; he broke it and gave it to them, saying: Take, eat; this is my body which is given for you; do this in remembrance of me.
All: Father, we do this in remembrance of him: his body is the bread of life.
Leader: At the end of supper, taking the cup of wine, he gave you thanks, and said: Drink this, all of you;

this is my blood of the new covenant, which is shed for you for the forgiveness of sins; do this in remembrance of me.

All: Father, we do this in remembrance of him: his blood is shed for all.

Leader: As we proclaim his death and celebrate his rising in glory, send your Holy Spirit that this bread and this wine may be to us the body and blood of your dear Son.

All: As we eat and drink these holy gifts make us one in Christ, our risen Lord.

Leader: With your whole Church throughout the world we offer you this sacrifice of praise and lift our voice to join the eternal song of heaven:

All: Holy, holy, holy Lord, God of power and might, heaven and earth are full of your glory. Hosanna in the highest.

FROM *COMMON WORSHIP*

✣

Appendix Two

Templates

All the templates and texts in Appendix Two can also be downloaded free of charge from the *Barnabas* website:
www.barnabasinchurches.org.uk/creativecommunion

U-turn arrow (red)

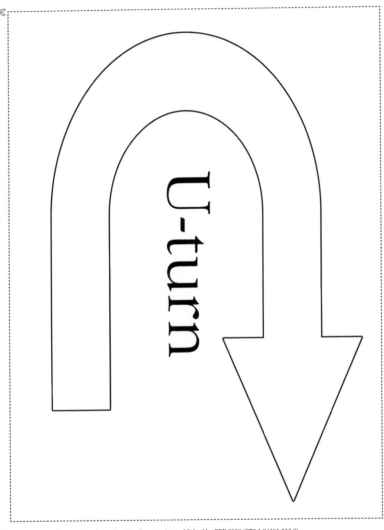

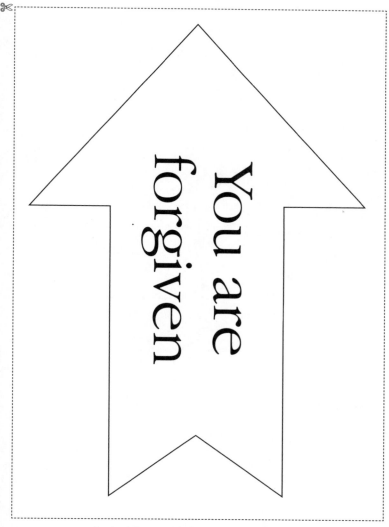

Forgiveness arrow (white)

Body of Christ place mat

Our bodies don't have just one part. They have many parts... But God has put all parts of our body together in the way that he decided is best...

It takes many parts to make a single body. That's why the eyes cannot say they don't need the hands. That's also why the head cannot say it doesn't need the feet. In fact, we cannot get along without the parts of the body that seem to be the weakest. We take special care to dress up some parts of our bodies. We are modest about our personal parts, but we don't have to be modest about other parts.

FROM 1 CORINTHIANS 12

The body of Christ has many different parts, just as any other body does. Some of us are Jews, and others are Gentiles. Some of us are slaves, and others are free. But God's Spirit baptized each of us and made us part of the body of Christ. Now we each drink from that same Spirit...

God put our bodies together in such a way that even the parts that seem the least important are valuable. He did this to make all parts of the body work together smoothly, with each part caring about the others. If one part of our body hurts, we hurt all over. If one part of our body is honoured, the whole body will be happy.

Body parts template

Body parts template

Cardboard body template

'Ten healthy choices' game board

43	44	45	46	47	48	49
42	41	40	39	38	37	36
29	30	31	32	33	34	35
28	27	26	25	24	23	22
15	16	17	18	19	20	21
14	13	12	11	10	9	8
1	2	3	4	5	6	7

Prayer card template

Lord God, I offer to you everything
that I am and everything I do.
    Especially today, I want to give…

_____

_____

_____

Help me this week to give my best
to you.

Seder meal script cards

Mother:
(*Lighting the candles*) Blessed are you, O Lord our God, king of the universe. You have chosen each one of us, and made us holy. In your name we light these lights. Blessed be God for ever!

Youngest child:
Why is this meal different? Why do we only eat unleavened bread on this night?

Child 2:
Why do we eat only bitter herbs on this night?

Child 3:
Why do we eat standing up?

Child 4:
Why do we eat lamb?

Child 5:
Why is Jesus called the Lamb of God?

Pizza wheels

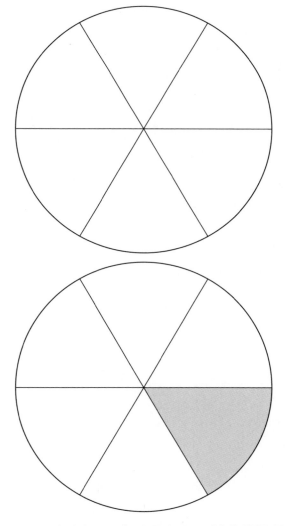

Grace cube

For every cup and
plateful, Lord,
make us truly
grateful.

For health and
strength and daily
food, we praise
your name, O
Lord.

May he who
blessed the loaves
and fishes bless
this family and
these dishes.

Thank you, Lord,
for this food.
Amen

Bless this bunch as
they munch their
lunch.

God our Father,
God our Father,
once again,
once again,
thank you
for our food.

✣

Appendix Three

Further reading

General books on the Eucharist

Celebrating the Eucharist, Ben Gordon-Taylor & Simon Jones (SPCK, 2004)
Dare to Break Bread, Geoffrey Howard (DLT, 1992)
Enriching the Liturgy, John Young (SPCK, 1998)
House of God, House of the People of God, Robin Gibbons (SPCK, 2005)
Liturgical Worship, Mark Earey (CHP, 2002)
Living Liturgy, John Leach (Kingsway, 1997)
Living the Eucharist, ed. Stephen Conway (DLT, 2001)
Mass Culture, ed. Pete Ward (BRF, 1999)
The Rite Stuff, ed. Pete Ward (BRF, 2004)
The Shape of the Liturgy, Dom Gregory Dix (Continuum, 2005)
Mission-Shaped Parish, Tim Sledge, Paul Bayes et al. (CHP, 2006)
Liturgy for Living, Charles Price & Louis Weil (Morehouse Publishing, 2000)
Re-Pitching the Tent, Richard Giles (Canterbury Press, 2006)
Creating Uncommon Worship, Richard Giles (Canterbury Press, 2006)

Children and the Eucharist

Let the Children Come to Communion, Stephen Lake (SPCK, 2006)
Living Liturgy, John Leach (Kingsway, 1997)
Mass Culture, ed. Pete Ward (BRF, 1999)
Mission-Shaped Children, Margaret Withers (CHP, 2006)

My Communion Book, Diana Murrie (CHP, 2002)
Table Talk, Donald Hilton (URC, 1998)
The Communion Cube, Diana Murrie & Margaret Withers (CHP, 2002)
The Rite Stuff, ed. Pete Ward (BRF, 2004)
Top Tips on All Age Worship, Nick Harding (SU, 2005)
Unless You Become Like This Child, Hans Urs von Balthasar (Ignatius, 1991)
Welcome to the Lord's Table revised edition, Margaret Withers (Barnabas, 2006)
Welcome to the Lord's Table activity book, Margaret Withers (Barnabas, 1999)
Youth Emmaus, Stephen Cottrell, Tim Sledge et al. (CHP, 2003)
Youth Emmaus 2, Tim Sledge, Sue Mayfield et al. (CHP, 2006)

Recipes from the emerging world

The Usborne Internet-linked Children's World Cookbook, Fiona Watt (Usborne, 2004)
The Usborne Little Round the World Cookbook, Angela Wilkes & Fiona Watt (Usborne, 2004)
Recipes for Disaster... Relief and Development, Gordon & Brenda Wilkinson (Available from tearfund@felbridge.com, 2006)
World Food Café 2: Easy Vegetarian Recipes from Around the Globe, Chris & Carolyn Caldicott (Frances Lincoln, 2006)

Notes

1 *Guidelines on the Admission of Baptised Persons to Holy Communion before Confirmation*, GS Misc 488 (1997).
2 Richard Giles, *How to Be an Anglican* (Canterbury Press, 2003).
3 Stephen Lake, *Let the Children Come to Communion* (SPCK, 2006), p. 111.
4 *Let the Children Come to Communion*, chapters 1—3
5 Margaret Withers, *Welcome to the Lord's Table* revised edition (Barnabas, 2006), sections 1–4.
6 *The Gospel according to Roly* (DVD: £10.99; video: £11.99), www.rolybain.co.uk.
7 *Jesus of Nazareth*, dir. Franco Zeffirelli (Carlton, 1977).
8 ed. Michael Perry, *The Dramatised Bible* (Marshall Pickering, 1997).
9 *Welcome to the Lord's Table,* Chapter 5 ('Preparation and resources').
10 *Welcome to the Lord's Table,* Chapter 3 ('What sort of people do we need?').
11 For example, Diane Simone Vezza and Susan Greenstein, *Passport on a Plate* (a round-the-world cook book for children) (Simon and Schuster, 1997); Angela Wilkes and Fiona Watt, *The Usborne Little Round the World Cookbook* (Children's cooking) (Usborne, 2004); Chris and Carolyn Caldicott, *World Food Café 2* (easy vegetarian recipes from around the globe) (Frances Lincoln, 2006).

Welcome to the Lord's Table

A practical course for preparing children to receive Holy Communion

Margaret Withers

This course is ideal for all who want to explore the implications of welcoming children to the Lord's Table.

Aimed primarily at clergy, children's workers, parents and teachers who want to enable children aged 7–9 to participate fully in eucharistic worship, the introductory chapters explore the background to the question of preparing young children for Holy Communion, give guidance on preparing the congregation, training leaders and involving the family, and include a guide to using the course.

The course itself comprises ten flexible teaching units plus four punctuation points to mark the journey. The material is designed to last approximately three months overall, with the children receiving Holy Communion towards the end of the course.

A task-based activity book is available separately to help the child make a personal record of his or her progress through the course.

Leader's course book: ISBN 978 1 84101 504 4 £12.99
Activity book: ISBN 978 1 84101 044 1 £3.99

Available from your local Christian bookshop or direct from BRF.
*Visit our website: **www.brf.org.uk***